PHARMACEUTICAL SALES FOR PHOOLS

THE BEGINNERS GUIDE FOR MEDICAL SALES REPRESENTATIVES

Sahil Syed

Published 2006 by arima publishing

www.arimapublishing.com

ISBN 1 84549 117 3

Printed and bound in the United Kingdom

Typeset in Bookman Old Style 12/16

arima publishing
ASK House, Northgate Avenue
Bury St Edmunds, Suffolk IP32 6BB
t: (+44) 01284 700321

www.arimapublishing.com

"The NHS is Europes largest employer and somehow Medical Representatives have to try and piece this customer jigsaw together - Pharmaceutical Sales for Phools uses easy language to help readers understand how the job works and how you can be successful. It is the perfect read – not only for those who are trying to get into the industry, but also for experienced representatives who just want to keep up to date on the mechanics of the job. From a Recruitment perspective this book is ideal for everyone to read in order to get to grips with the pharmaceutical industry, and how it attempts to work with the NHS. This book will compliment companies' training courses and will give trainee representatives a lot of confidence when going onto Initial Training Course which is so important. The pragmatic approach by the author, and the use of everyday language makes it essential reading"

**Niall Barry - Director,
Gem Resourcing**

Niall has over 22 years' experience in the pharmaceutical industry and service sector, much of which has been focussed in recruitment.

Niall has spent recent times conducting personal research with sales representatives through a number of field visits, and has also attended various exhibitions to consolidate this knowledge. Through this work Niall has met an array of NHS specialists, PCT personnel, and industry regional managers. This has given Niall an in-depth and up-to-date knowledge of what is happening at ground level within the NHS and the pharmaceutical industry.

Niall has successfully launched Gem Resourcing as a highly innovative recruitment company which offers a totally candidate focussed service for pharmaceutical industry candidates. Gem resourcing offers candidates the opportunity to look at specific job openings on-line, and to talk to recruitment specialists about suitable positions.

For further information about Gem Resourcing, see appendix

"Pharmaceutical Sales for Phools provides a truly comprehensive review of the role of the medical representative. This is the first example I have seen of a common sense approach to the job which leaves nothing to the imagination, it should provide a very useful addition to traditional training methods for people entering the industry"

**Charles Marshall - Director,
Axis Development**

With an academic background in Psychology and Economics and a professional background in sales and marketing, Charles Marshall has spent the last 18 years in a variety of management positions.

A great deal of this has concentrated upon the development of individuals within organisations and the creation and maintenance of effective teams.

Charles' experience within the pharmaceutical industry has also led to a high awareness of the issues currently facing the NHS. This has led to Charles becoming the co-founder of Axis Development, an organisation designed to supply a wider range of concomitant skills to healthcare professionals.

Highly influenced by modern management ideology, his main focus is on personal development, performance and achievement by developing successful strategies and attitudes.

"This book is a bible for medical sales representatives entering the industry, and even for those (like myself) who are experienced. If I'd have had something like this when I first started, I would have become much more productive, much more quickly. It is indispensable – every representative should have a copy"

Gary Fagg
Principle Sales Representative,
Novartis Pharmaceuticals

With over 30 years experience in primary care sales, Gary Fagg is amongst the most skilled and well respected medical sales representatives in the industry.

Gary joined Bayer in 1973 and enjoyed 28 successful years where he was consistently in the top 5 sales performers list. He later became one of the first 5 associates ever to reach executive representative status at Bayer.

In 2001 he took early retirement, but was then tempted back into sales when he was recruited by Novartis in 2002 as a senior representative. It then took just 12 months for Gary to once again achieve the accolade of Principal Representative with Novartis.

Dedication

*I dedicate this book to the memory
of my dear grandmother. Someone
who was a ray of light in our family,
for the fact that she showed unconditional
love to every generation, and every
individual that she touched.*

Forever in our hearts.....

'Nani'
Dr. Afroz Jahan
1919 - 2006

CONTENTS

PART 2. UNDERSTANDING YOUR ROLE

PART 3. PUTTING IT ALL TOGETHER – YOUR FIRST THREE MONTHS ON TERRITORY

PART 4. APPENDIX

ACKNOWLEDGEMENTS

In my time I have had the pleasure of working with some very special individuals who have either given me knowledge, support or inspiration – each in their own unique ways. I therefore wish to acknowledge them here; To my old manager David James who gave me my first break into this great industry. To Jayshree Patel, my longest serving area manager who has supported me for many of my best years in the industry. To Nicola Brown – the lady who trained me for my first journey into the pharma industry and made it so much fun! To Andy Peltz – my old partner in crime, with whom I shared some great times during my early years.

To Inderjeet Veghal – the man who came in as my 'rookie' territory partner, and then proceeded to blow me and everyone else out of the water with his performances! To Gary Fagg – A *true* salesperson, and the owner of the most brutal line bending sales graphs I have ever seen in pharmaceuticals! To Ahmed Elhusseiny – without doubt, the brightest and most talented associate who I am privileged enough to have worked alongside, a man who truly inspired me – '*particularly in the club*!'.

To Zoe Chambers – one third of the old '4610' dream-team, with whom I have shared some of my most enjoyable times in the primary care arena. Also, to Bindu Paliwal. Firstly because she made up the remaining third of our dream-team, but also because she is someone who has demonstrated unrivalled focus for her goals, and has done so in the most professional manner of anyone I have known in this industry.

I wish to acknowledge my mother Dr. Sitara Syed who of course has given me support – not only in my formative years of writing this book, but in my formative years of becoming a human being! To my brother in law Ahmet -

my first true mentor who helped to open my eyes to the realities of 'dealing with people'.

I cannot complete this book without mentioning my two children – Neji and Dilara. Not least because of the innocent pride and excitement which they have expressed at the idea that 'Baba' has been writing his own book, but as much because they are at the heart of why I work as hard as I do.

Also, my brother Owais Syed has always been someone who I have looked up to - not only as an older brother, but also as a pharma industry role model. He has enjoyed a very successful career in this industry in his own right, and it has been inspiring for me to have seen *his* professional growth in parallel with my own development.

Of the many people around me, there are very few whom I would have trusted and valued enough to have had a *significant* input into the content of this book. I therefore wish to acknowledge Owais – firstly because he duly stepped up to this role, but secondly because he then gave so much to it with true belief, and true backing. Together, Owais and I single-handedly took on the roles of becoming the focus group, the steering committee *and* the editorial panel for this entire book.

The idea for this book first came to me when *I myself* was brand new to the industry. It then lay dormant in my mind until four years ago when I was first inspired to turn a tatty spider-gram of random ideas into a tangible manuscript of some sort. In reality, due to the amount of priorities I manage in my life, it could have taken me a decade to have completed this book.

Therefore, and most importantly, I wish to acknowledge my wife Zali, because you - more than anyone else, have given me the opportunity to make this vision of mine become a reality. You have helped me manage my time, offered unconditional support throughout this entire project, and have always given me encouragement when I needed it. You are my rock and you mean the world to me.

In truth, the fact that this book has taken so long to create means that I have inevitably had to sacrifice many precious hours with both my wife *and* my children. Their collective tolerance has been infinite - therefore making this piece of work as much their's as my own.

ABOUT THE AUTHOR

Sahil Syed has worked in pharmaceutical sales for over seven years during which time he has worked with some of the largest global pharmaceutical companies in the world. In this time he has achieved promotions to senior sales representative and to hospital specialist representative. In 2002 he won a national CEO award for leading key customer initiatives, prior to being selected as one of only 12 associates to become part of a UK advanced sales academy. He has also been trained for a leadership role at one of the most prestigious management academies in the UK.

In addition to these achievements Sahil has been selected to work on a number of internal projects which has given him insight and first hand exposure into sales management, sales training, pharma marketing and the NHS structure itself.

Sahil Syed,
Author

ABOUT THIS BOOK

WHY PHARMACEUTICAL SALES FOR PHOOLS?

In deciding where I wanted to go with this book I have had to be very careful as to where I draw my boundaries, because this entire topic could be infinite with opinions and debates. There are currently *some* texts relating to the pharmaceutical industry which are already available – they have pre-dominantly been developed for the US market however.

In contrast, *Pharmaceutical Sales for Phools* has been written with specific reference to those factors which affect pharmaceutical sales across the UK – namely the pressures on brand prescribing, the influencing power of drug formularies at various levels of the NHS and the implementation of the NHS specific initiatives such as the new General Medical Services contract for GPs. Many of these issues will obviously not have been covered in the American texts, yet they are having an increasing influence on drug prescribing.

There are also a number of different processes and policies in both the NHS *and* the pharmaceutical industry in the UK. You will find that customers and colleagues alike will use a range of colloquial terms to describe these entities. Because of this, I found that a large proportion of my early career was spent trying to decipher this 'industry-speak', since no one ever took the time to explain the bare basics of what they all meant, what their significance was and therefore how they all inter-linked to form the 'big-picture'. New representatives will invariably have many questions upon entering the industry - *What is a PCT? What is a formulary? What is a prescribing budget, and what exactly, influences prescribing behaviour?*

The other issue with most pharmaceutical sales books currently available, is that too many of them seem to focus on *'how to get your foot in the door'* of the industry. Their emphasis tends to be on networking, generating job offers and managing pharmaceutical job interviews. Whilst I agree that such information *is* extremely useful to aspiring candidates, I believe that there are still some fundamental questions which need to be understood in relation to the role itself. *How is the pharmaceutical sales role different to other sales roles? Why is it that some customers will see pharmaceutical representatives and others won't? Where would I start when I am new?*

What this book aims to do is to answer these very questions and many more in a systematic, easy-to-read format. The aim is to fill these basic knowledge gaps for *aspiring* candidates, and therefore to serve as a reference/support tool for *established* representatives too.

AUTHOR'S NOTE

During my time in industry I have been continually challenged in my role and this has kept me as interested in the job today, as when I first started. When I did first join however, I struggled to find any such book which could give me a robust understanding of all of the basic elements of this industry. I therefore know that there is a genuine need for such a book.

What makes Pharmaceutical Sales for Phools unique is that I have exclusively written this book based on my own experiences of the industry, which means that what you read in this book really is how you will see things out in the field.

DISCLAIMER/EXPLANATORY NOTES

The information contained within this book has been collated and expressed solely by Sahil Syed, and as such the views and opinions put forward do not necessarily represent the views of the ABPI, the NHS or of any of the organisations which Sahil Syed has worked for, or mentioned within this book. The disclaimer also extends to the commentators who have critically reviewed this book.

Readers should note that throughout the book doctors will be referred to as 'he', and representatives and sales professionals will be referred to as 'she'. This is purely done in order to aid readers in distinguishing between the two roles that are continually referred to within the text, and is in no way intended to be discriminatory.

It goes without saying that both doctors and pharmaceutical sales professionals can of course be both male and female, and the nomenclature which has been used is in no way representative of the actual male-female distribution in either industry.

A glossary of terms and abbreviations has also been collated at the end of the book. This is designed to help readers who may not be familiar with the abbreviations which have been used at various points within the text.

INTRODUCTION

New representatives starting a career in selling to health service professionals may have many fears about the role. The thought of discussing medicines with highly qualified, experienced doctors is understandably daunting – not to mention the fact that your aim with these professionals is to actually *alter* their prescribing practice, rather than just 'discuss' medicines with them.

However, there are hundreds of pharmaceutical companies, and thousands of medical representatives operating in the UK in a role which has come to be regarded as a fundamental success factor for multinational pharmaceutical companies.

The unusual dynamic of drug prescribing means that whilst doctors use medicines as central tools in their never-ending fight to control diseases and illnesses, they will never have to go out and 'purchase' medicines themselves. This means that a knowledgeable professional from the pharmaceutical sector is inherently required to *seek-out* the prescriber in *their* habitat, and carry the sales discussion to them – hence the birth of the medical sales representative – a critical, yet often misunderstood stakeholder operating in the sphere of medical care.

PART 1

BACKGROUND

1. WHY BECOME A MEDICAL REPRESENTATIVE?

If you have taken the step to read this book then you will undoubtedly have been exposed to *some* hook that has captured your interest to want to investigate the job further.

In my opinion and my experience, there are three key reasons why anyone does a job - and I mean ANYONE! I therefore propose my theory of *'the three cornerstones of employment';*

1. **Salary/bonuses/benefits**. Within this heading, the extra perks which have monetary value such as a company car, pension scheme and medical insurance would also be included
2. **Job satisfaction**. i.e. to what extent do you actually *enjoy* the job you do on a day to day basis, regardless of what the pay is? (Within this category I would also regard job security as a factor)
3. **Career development**. Is this job helping you to develop a skill for a *future* aspired role? (i.e. your current job may not pay particularly well, it may not be the most satisfying, but you may nonetheless be doing it to learn a necessary skill in preparation for your next career move).

In this way you can see that people would either do a job for any one, or any *combination* of the above needs. The point is that if not even a *single* one of these elements is being fulfilled, you will probably feel it is time to move on. Consequently, if a job can actually fulfil any (or ideally ALL) of these requirements then of course, it will be more desirable.

The reason why I have presented this theory is that I believe the pharmaceutical industry (through the role of the medical representative) can offer fulfilment in *all three* of the cornerstones.

Firstly, relative to many other industries, the salary and benefits are excellent. At the time of this book going to print, I would estimate that a university graduate going into a full time position as a headcount representative can start on a basic salary of approximately £18,000 per year, plus entry into a bonus scheme. From here I know of long serving 'career representatives' who are earning over £45,000 per year in a GP sales role (though this of course will only come with *many* years of experience and with significant, proven sales success).

In addition to the financial return, will come the extra perks which will typically include a fully expensed company car, entry into a company pension scheme, personal medical insurance, approximately twenty five days paid annual leave, paid sick leave, paid maternity/paternity leave and access into a preference share scheme. There may be further benefits offered, but these will then vary from one company to the next.

In terms of job satisfaction, there is undoubtedly going to be a constant challenge within this role. A cynic could argue that 'challenge' may mean different things to different people which is a fair point. It is my belief however, that this job is so dynamic and fast moving in so many ways, that this provides us with a continuously stimulating work challenge. For example, companies will evolve their tactical plans year by year, customer environments often change and competitors offer challenges of their own – there really isn't room for those who seek a mundane 'nine-to-five' job!

Another major benefit which keeps many representatives attracted to the job is the fact that they are mobile ('field based') and not stuck in an office! Along with this, the job offers considerable flexibility of working hours. It is important however to interpret this point correctly, because whilst this *is* a very true benefit, it *doesn't* represent one of the old myths of the job which I discuss in the next chapter (i.e. that representatives see a few doctors in the morning and the day's work is then finished!) How this flexibility *does* manifest itself is in the autonomy which you are given to be able to manage your own working schedule.

That is, whilst your overall objectives and parameters *will* be very specifically set, the way in which you plan and shape your day to day customer contacts *are* very much in your own hands. For example, you can choose to make the bulk of your customer contacts either in the early, late or mid morning. Alternatively, you may want to spread them equally *throughout* the day. The point is, so long as you meet the minimum daily activity requirements, you *will* have the flexibility to choose what suits you. In this way you can spend the rest of your time planning and facilitating other aspects of the job in a way which allows you to maximise your time management.

In terms of job security, the pharmaceutical industry certainly has flourished in the past few decades, and the realisation that salespeople are the most effective way to generate sales growth really has been proven during this time.

Admittedly, the lucrative industry growth which was seen particularly in the 80's and 90's, *has* slowed in recent years, but this is mainly due to the fact that many of the mega-brand drugs of this era such as Losec, Istin, Zantac, Zestril, Innovace and Prozac have *all* lost their product patents. These were all true blockbuster products which generated tens of millions of pounds in sales for their respective manufacturers. Of course, these sales are now predominantly being consumed by generic drug manufacturers (a full discussion of this subject is given in chapter 7).

It is important to remember that the long term security of pharmaceutical companies is determined by the potential success of drugs which are currently in development stages – a concept in pharmaceuticals which is referred to as the strength of the 'product-pipeline'.

To give readers an indication of how difficult it is for a product to actually come to market, it is worth noting that for each drug which is successfully launched by a manufacturer, tens and possibly hundreds of others will have failed at some stage of their development, e.g. due to safety concerns, or a lack of effectiveness.

Therefore in an effort to try and reduce the risk of development products failing to reach the market, many drug companies have chosen to merge in recent years. The benefit of this strategy is that individual organisations are able to consolidate their respective strengths. This will maximise the growth potential beyond that which either of the individual companies would otherwise achieve if they were to operate alone. Companies such as Glaxo, SmithKline Beecham, Astra, Zeneca, Sanofi and Aventis have all gone through such mergers in recent years.

Another related concept is that of acquisitions. As the name suggests, this is when a large pharmaceutical company buys out a smaller, often research-based company for the purpose of acquiring a desirable product at development stage. This creates a mutually beneficial situation:

- The *large* company is obtaining a product at a (usually) more advanced stage of development, without incurring the vast risk and expense normally associated with such products.

- The *smaller* company is able to draw upon the established sales and distribution channels which these larger companies have invariably built up. This enables the smaller company to realise its objective of marketing the new drug to as wide a clinician base as possible.

Despite the need for such mergers and acquisitions, the vast number of new drugs which are nonetheless being discovered and developed means that the pharmaceutical industry continues to prosper. So what does this mean for the job security of medical representatives?

Well, whilst mergers and acquisitions invariably *do* result in job losses at various departmental levels, I am still a strong believer that for the foreseeable future it would take a catastrophic disaster to the pharmaceutical industry for the role of the medical representative to disappear completely.

Yes - redundancies *will* happen, but due to the undeniable influence which pharmaceutical sales representatives have on generating sales growth, it would be counter-productive for pharmaceutical companies to completely slash this branch of their businesses. It is my strong personal belief therefore, that there will *always* be a need for pharmaceutical sales representatives in some capacity.

The final consideration of my cornerstones theory is the need for skills consolidation, leading to career development. I have seen first hand that the pharmaceutical industry offers superb personal development – both within the role of a medical representative, *and* in preparation for bigger and better roles within pharmaceutical companies. I believe that the pharmaceutical industry offers *truly* meritocratic opportunities for development to those individuals who prove successful within their roles.

Within the sales function those medical representatives who can demonstrate a track record of consistent sales growth along with high personal competence, can progress into a number of specialised sales roles such as:

- *Senior Medical Representative* – This role is essentially similar to that of the medical representative, but the title reflects exceptional levels of competence and success which have been demonstrated within the role. A senior representative may well be given extra responsibilities in view of their recognised ability. They may also be given small perks such as company car upgrades
- The final progressive step on from the Senior Representative, is that of a *Principal, or Executive Medical Representative* – This role has a similar profile to that of the *Senior* representative, but this represents the absolute pinnacle of achievement within the medical representative sales role. It is highly regarded, and relatively exclusive. You will usually have to demonstrate *exceptional* success both as a medical representative, *and then* as a senior representative before you can reach this level (it should also be noted that some companies use this nomenclature interchangeably, and so 'executive' may also refer to the next step up from a medical representative, and 'senior' may represent the highest level as previously described)
- *Hospital Representatives* are responsible for liaising exclusively with hospital consultants and other hospital professionals. Their three

broad responsibilities are to secure hospital formulary inclusions, to drive sales within hospital units (for 'in-patients') and to drive product referrals for community 'out-patients'

- *Healthcare Development Managers (HDMs).* These professionals are responsible for working with key decision makers at PCT level in order to try and develop local policies/guidelines endorsing the use of your promoted products. (PCTs are discussed in chapter 6, and policies/guidelines are explained in chapter 10).

If a move away from direct 'customer-facing' roles are desired, then the following progressive positions are amongst the most popular;

- *Training Executives* – who are responsible for training and coaching sales representatives on product knowledge, and selling skills models. They may also be involved in the design and development of representative training programmes, including the mandatory new starters' 'initial training course' (or ITC).
- *Regional Business Managers (or RBMs)* who are responsible for managing a team of sales representatives – usually around 6-12 (though the exact numbers can vary). Their main job description would be to lead and manage a team of sales representatives to achieve targets which they are set for both sales and contact rates. Interestingly, many commentators regard the job of the RBM as being the most important and therefore often the most challenging in the industry.
- Head office based *Marketing Executives* who are responsible for developing and delivering marketing campaigns, looking after market

research and providing salesforce support in promoting products.

It goes without saying that each of these roles will come with greater work challenges, greater personal development through further training, and of course greater remuneration.

In *direct* relation to the essence of the third cornerstone, it is clear that selling is a universal skill which can be utilised in a variety of situations. Selling is something which needs to be applied in customer interactions, and no less with internal colleagues in business environments where you may be selling, and championing an idea to your *own team* for example. Therefore to learn how to sell, is clearly a vital key to success – whether it be as a medical representative or in any other role.

As I have therefore said, in the context of my proposed theory of the three cornerstones of employment, a career in pharmaceutical sales can definitely offer fulfilment in each of the three areas.

2. BUSTING THE MYTHS OF THE INDUSTRY

1. *"YOU NEED TO HAVE A SCIENCE DEGREE TO BECOME A MEDICAL REPRESENTATIVE"*

Not true. Admittedly, in the past this often was the case but with the increased need for business and commercial awareness within this industry, candidates from a variety of backgrounds are being accepted into medical sales roles. The more pertinent questions nowadays tend to be *"Can you sell? Can you work in a team? Can you demonstrate business acumen?"*

I myself studied media, sociology and politics at college, and eventually graduated with an honours degree in business and marketing. When I was asked about how I felt this affected my chances of landing a pharmaceutical sales job, I simply explained that to be a car salesperson you do not need to be a mechanic, to be an estate agent you do not need to be an architect or a builder, so why did I need a medical degree to sell in pharmaceuticals? I put the argument to my prospective employers, that if I could prove I had basic awareness of business and commerce, then *surely* they should be able to teach me the science side of the job? Of course, the rest is history!

2. *"THE WORKING DAY OF A MEDICAL REP ONLY CONSISTS OF SEEING A HANDFUL OF DOCTORS – THE REST IS FREE TIME"*

Because of the fact that most GPs operate surgeries hours between around 8am to 1pm, this is also *the* time therefore, in which representatives will be seeing their GP customers (i.e. their *main* target customers). It is therefore assumed by many, that since customer calls are the key element of a salesperson's job, that medical representatives aren't really working the rest of the time.

In actual fact this job is very unique in that the amount of training, preparation and planning time that goes into coordinating your sales calls, far outweighs the *actual* selling time which you will have in front of your customers. The reason that this myth exists therefore, is that in any other sales role the vast majority of a sales representatives time is actually spent as selling time in front of their clients.

With pharmaceutical representatives, what actually takes place after the GP visits is the start of the pharmacy calls, the practice manager calls, territory planning meetings, call reporting, meeting preparations, e-mailing and other administration (to name just a few things!) The point is that whilst the GP calls are of course the 'bread and butter' of the job, the role has become so specialised now that in order to get the most out of these visits, so much more actually needs to go into the call planning beforehand. This is why this belief really is a myth!

3. *"DRUG REPS ARE SIMPLY PAID TO DRIVE AROUND IN COMPANY CARS AND TAKE DOCTORS OUT TO DINNER!"*

Yes of course we are! And the prime minister is paid to live in a fancy house in Westminster! (Let's just forget about the fact that he probably has the greatest job pressure of anyone else in this country). But let's not forget about David Beckham who is loved by millions of fans and who can afford to drive around in an array of expensive sports cars!

In reality of course, David Beckham probably feels immeasurable pressure when he is about to take a penalty kick in front of millions of spectators. And what about the constant media intrusion into *every* aspect of his *entire* life?

What I am getting at of course, is that just like any other job there are of course high points and perks within our job, but these can often mask the pressure, intensity and accountability that also comes with the role of a medical representative.

In reality the car (for example) is just an essential tool required for the job since it really does become a representatives 'mobile-office'. In terms of the dinners - well these are by no means intended as jolly affairs of eating and drinking. It is an ABPI rule that *every* medical meeting should have a clear educational content, and that the offer of dinner and drinks to healthcare professionals must *always* be secondary to the educational purpose of the meeting[1]. Therefore dinner meetings are as much a professional part of the job as any other promotional activity.

4. *"DOCTORS ACCEPT PAYMENTS AND GIFTS FROM DRUG COMPANIES IN RETURN FOR PRESCRIBING THEIR PRODUCTS...."*

Many industry-naïve people feel that drug companies offer pens, stationery and other small gifts as a direct enticement to prescribe medicines. It *is* true that drug companies do produce modest giveaways such as pens, pads, diaries etc, but to think that doctors would *really* prescribe drugs in exchange for such superfluous items is quite ludicrous.

The existence of the ABPI itself further reinforces the redundancy of this argument. As I will go on to describe in chapter 4, the ABPI operates a very strict code of conduct which regulates the promotional activities of drug companies. This is to ensure that they conduct business in an ethical way, which means avoiding any practices that will gain the company an unfair competitive advantage. Pharmaceutical companies now

---

[1] *'Code of Practice for the Pharmaceutical Industry'* 2006 – Prescription Medicines Code of Practice Authority: www.pmcpa.org.uk

more than ever, are taking such self regulation extremely seriously.

UK ABPI guidelines actually state that any promotional item given to a doctor or their staff must be inexpensive (not exceeding a value of £6.00) and also, the item's functional purpose *must* be directly relevant to the recipients profession[1].

Even from the doctors' viewpoint however, the threat of patient litigation is currently very topical within the NHS – this is a situation where a patient files a legal claim against a doctor in a case of medical negligence which they believe has lead to illness, further complications or even death. I challenge you to ask ANY doctor in the UK today if the potential threat of such action does not cross their mind at some time. The ultimate implication of such legal proceedings is that the GP can be 'struck-off' the medical register, which means that they will lose their license to practice medicine and ultimately therefore, their livelihood.

Also, as part of the relatively new GP appraisal and revalidation process in the UK, GPs must demonstrate to health authority appraisers that they exercise probity (i.e. integrity) in ALL financial dealings of their work. (The GP appraisal and revalidation process actually grants a doctor his continued license to practice medicine). Therefore with such intense focus on this area of medicine it is *extremely* rare in this day and age to find *any* GP who would prescribe drugs inappropriately, based on unethical enticements from the pharmaceutical industry (or anyone else).

---

[1]*'Code of Practice for the Pharmaceutical Industry'* 2006 – Prescription Medicines Code of Practice Authority: www.pmcpa.org.uk

3. 'COMPLETING A SALE' – HOW IT WORKS IN PHARMACEUTICALS

Traditional sales processes are fairly easy to conceptualise. Imagine a chocolate bar sales rep. She sells the benefit of her product to her customer (for example a convenience store owner), who then makes an immediate order for an agreed volume of the product. The rep knows *there and then* what level of sales she has generated from the sales call, as the transaction is effectively 'rubber stamped' on the spot.

The sales success of a medical representative is unfortunately a little more complex to track! Initially your sales interaction could be very much like that of the chocolate bar rep. That is, by using basic selling processes (probing, selling to customer needs etc.) you could convince your customer that your product is the one to 'buy' (i.e. that your drug is the one that should be prescribed instead of a competitors).

The challenge in pharmaceuticals is that product sales are 'patient-opportunity driven'. This means that unlike the convenience store owner who will bulk-purchase a product in readiness for customer consumption, a doctor will only prescribe a product as and when an ill patient presents to them. Therefore you as the medical representative will have to conclude your sales deal with (at best) a verbal commitment from the doctor that he will prescribe your drug when the next relevant opportunity presents itself.

From then on, there is no absolute way of determining whether or not the doctor has carried through the commitment, and therefore no way of you knowing if your selling interaction with the customer was successful. (Unlike the chocolate bar sales rep who walks away with a signed order for a definite volume of stock). The only exception to this rule may be dispensing practice agreements which do require 'dotted-line' type agreements resulting in bulk stock buying.

In light of these complexities, medical representatives are forced to use some of the following tactics to determine their sales progress;

- Representatives can analyse local sales data* - although this will usually only correlate to a 'brick' (postal code), or to clusters of practices at best - *not* to a specific GP. This aggregated data may confirm a positive sales trend which can either be the result of an *individual* GPs significant increase in prescribing, or the result of *several* GPs each prescribing a moderate amount of units. Representatives should then use any or all of the following methods to try and ascertain which of these is the case.
- Representatives may have an informal chat with the local pharmacist to find out if there have been any new prescriptions coming through from particular GPs (see section on community pharmacists, in chapter 16)
- Representatives may talk with the GP's own practice nurse who may be willing to let you know if the GP has prescribed the drug
- Finally, you could of course ask the doctor himself in the next call whether or not he has prescribed your product. As for how honest he is with you though, is purely down to his discretion!

* *Regional Sales Analysis (or RSA) is the most commonly used set of sales data in the pharmaceutical industry.*

Another complexity to consider is that your sales success (as measured by the majority of pharma companies) will be how much of your product is ordered by *pharmacies, not* by how much a doctor actually prescribes. That is, if a doctor were to prescribe your product to 10 patients but theoretically none of them took their prescription to a pharmacy, then you would not be recognised for these sales in any way (again, this definition is not true for representatives who deal with dispensing practices, or even for vaccine representatives who are also responsible for taking direct orders with customers).

Figure 1 describes how this process works whereby the solid arrows represent the flow of demand for a drug, and the dotted arrow represents the point at which these transactions are picked-up in the local sales data (i.e. RSA) which has been described above. The sales are then attributed back to a local representative by 'geographical default'.

Another challenge which this therefore presents, is that of 'floating/migrating scripts' which can also disguise true sales attainment. This is a concept whereby prescriptions which are written by a doctor on *another* geographical sales territory may be dispensed by a pharmacy on *your* territory which will result in you being unfairly credited with a sale. I once encountered this scenario while covering a Central London territory. Pharmacies situated near busy railway stations would dispense large quantities of my drug, via prescriptions which were written by GPs far outside my territory. This was due to commuters bringing their locally written scripts to have them conveniently dispensed by a pharmacy near their place of work.

Therefore, I was often being credited with sales which were probably generated by the work of representatives outside of my own territory. So whilst this may at first sound as if you will be achieving extra sales without extra effort, beware that the same scenario could also *conversely* affect you!

Such a scenario can also be a problem for those representatives who have target GPs practicing on the border of two separate sales territories, or indeed if the 'nearest' pharmacy is located just inside another territory.

The final issue with tracking pharmaceutical sales is the time lag which occurs from the point at which sales calls are made, to when sales data becomes available. This time lag will typically be 6-8 weeks in length. You are therefore constantly working with a time delay when trying to monitor your effectiveness, which means that the results of those activities which you undertake 'today', will only be available to analyse many weeks later.

Figure 1. Flow of a drug sale

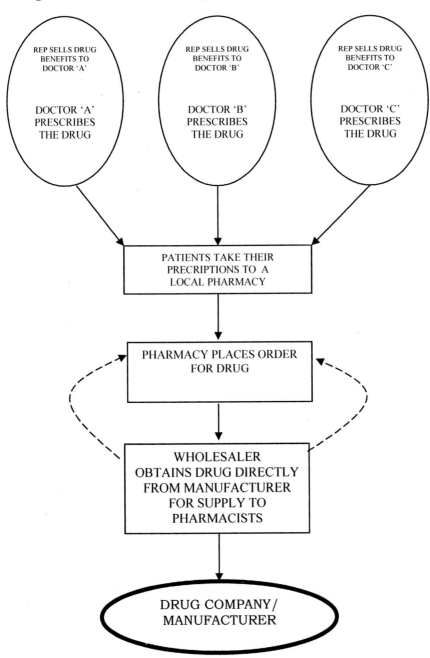

4. THE ABPI – *THE REPRESENTATIVE BODY OF PHARMACEUTICALS IN THE UK*

Companies in various industries will often choose to become part of an independent or self regulatory body of some sort. To become a member of such an organisation is sometimes a prerequisite rule of trading in a particular market, but membership may just as often be voluntary. Of course, the benefits of *voluntary* adherence to such authorities is that companies can demonstrate greater ethical intent since *technically*, they are not required to abide by their rules.

The Association of British Pharmaceutical Industries (ABPI) is the representative body of pharmaceutical industries in the UK. The ABPI operates a very specific code of conduct which dictates the ethical guidelines within which sales professionals and pharmaceutical companies as a whole, can conduct their promotional activities[1]. This code of practice is administered by the Prescription Medicines Code of Practice Authority (or PMCPA) – a distinct arm of the ABPI who were *specifically* set up to oversee the implementation of the code.

Just as The Advertising Standards Authority (ASA) and Office of Fair Trade (OFT) operate rules and guidelines in order to guide the fair trade of consumer goods to the general public, the ABPI defines rules which ensure that pharma companies and their sales staff do not pursue commercial gain at the expense of fair, legal and ethical influence of drug prescribers.

For example, as a sales representative you cannot deliberately misrepresent the results of a clinical study to make your products appear more effective than your competitor's products. A prescriber has the right to know

---

[1] *'Code of Practice for the Pharmaceutical Industry'* 2006 – Prescription Medicines Code of Practice Authority: www.pmcpa.org.uk

the exact results and conditions of *any* clinical trial in order for *them* to be able to make judgements on the interpretation of its results. Also, companies cannot use terms such as 'the best' or 'the safest' as these are regarded as exaggerated, all embracing superlatives which may inappropriately suggest that an active ingredient has some special merit, quality or property.

The list of rules and regulations outlined by the ABPI are extensive and the above examples simply indicate that there should be a clear and level playing field upon which any influencing can occur. Since we are ultimately dealing with ill patients in this industry, the implications of improper prescribing can obviously be fatal, so it is imperative that doctors should never be exposed to a situation where they are influenced into prescribing a drug where it is clinically inappropriate to do so.

Such is the importance of the ABPI code of practice, that it was recently subject to an in depth review which resulted in some key changes being made. These changes have become effective in 2006, and ultimately serve to enhance the overall conduct of pharmaceutical product promotion.

In order to comply with the code, the ABPI stipulates that representatives who are selling pharmaceutical medicines to doctors and other healthcare professionals should have a minimum standard of industry and clinical knowledge. This is because, as professional salespeople representing pharmaceutical companies, you are effectively ambassadors for the industry itself.

Therefore as part of your training as a medical sales representative you will be required to sit the ABPI's industry examination within the first year of your employment in the industry. You are then required to actually *pass* the examination within the first *two* years of your employment. Companies will usually pay the relevant fees for their representatives to undertake distance learning and to actually sit the examination itself. This obviously comes at some expense to companies but the majority of them accept this as part of cost of bringing new representatives up to the required standard of selling.

For those candidates who do *not* have a background of medical education, the ABPI examination tends to come as a *particularly* intense test. As I highlighted in chapter 2, my own educational background is completely non-medical so I too found that the level of scientific focus of the exam required me to put in a *significantly* greater effort before I became comfortable and conversant with it. Having done this once though, I did find that *any* medical material which I was subsequently required to absorb, was always far more easier to understand since the medical concepts and terminology became more and more familiar to me.

My advice to new representatives would be to try not to leave all your exam preparations to the last few weeks (as *so* many representatives seem to do!) Everyone around you will undoubtedly appreciate that you will have a lot of work to take on due to the exam preparations as well as having to get to grips with the new job itself. Despite this, it is very rare for companies to afford their representatives any significant study time. It is therefore clear that one way or another you will have to schedule study periods into your own working days, so pacing yourself is paramount to good preparation. Cramming this study time into a shorter time frame will only serve to pressure you more!

5. WHY DOCTORS MAY OR MAY NOT SEE REPRESENTATIVES

It is important to understand the reasons why some GPs will agree to see medical representatives and others will not. The need to understand this is twofold. Firstly, most companies will invariably set their representatives the task of seeing difficult-to-access GPs. It is therefore important to appreciate the thinking of such customers. Secondly, and most notably in my own experience, the motivation behind *why* a GP will agree to see a representative can largely dictate the nature of the call itself.

The issue of whether or not customers agree to see medical representatives may appear strange to some readers – especially those who have worked in a sales role before. This is because in other industries generally, if a customer needs to obtain a product then they would *have* to interact with a sales representative in order to discuss product details and then to formalise an order (for example with cars, furniture, double glazing etc). Our industry is quite unique in that a customer (i.e. a doctor) can readily use the products produced by pharmaceutical companies without ever having to liaise with a salesperson of any type.

Doctors can check product details via electronic or printed literature to determine important prescribing information such as doses, pack sizes and clinical uses for drugs. Therefore (as described in chapter 3) when a GP prescribes a product, an order will automatically be placed via a set of middle-men (i.e. the pharmacists and the wholesalers). The doctor's requirement would thereby be systematically met once the patients medicine is dispensed at a community pharmacy.

The real irony of this issue is that doctors actually need medicines as the main tools of their trade, and so without them, their ability to cure illnesses would be all but impossible!

You can therefore see that medical representatives have the challenges of not only needing to increase sales in some very competitive markets, but also of having to tackle the complexity of *how* to see customers to be able to influence this process.

During my time in pharmaceutical sales I have come across many reasons which doctors themselves have suggested as to why they may agree to see medical representatives. One interesting story was told to me by a GP in London. She told of how she never used to see representatives either in her practice or even when she trained in hospitals. However at a hospital meeting one day she came across a representative who was giving away new tourniquets (she really needed one as her own one had recently broke). That same afternoon she rushed to an emergency whilst on a home visit, and actually used that same tourniquet to save a patient from bleeding to death. From that day onwards, she has made it a point to try and see representatives whenever possible!

This is obviously an atypical story, though the following are some of the more standardised reasons which I will call the 'value-reasons' of why many GPs tend to see representatives;

'VALUE' REASONS WHY GPS MAY AGREE TO SEE REPRESENTATIVES

- To learn about new drugs and therefore to save them from having to seek out this information for themselves

- To learn about *new* indications for *existing* drugs
- To learn about the comparative efficacy of competitive products in a given class
- To gain simplified and summarised synopses of clinical trial results without having to read *entire* trials
- To enlist support from pharma companies via the various value added products or services which some of them offer - such as practice training, clinical auditing, accredited doctor training/educational programmes, or some of the many clinical items (such as the tourniquets mentioned above).

Interestingly, I have also seen the following being given as reasons for why GPs agree to see medical representatives. When GPs choose to see representatives for the following reasons, doctors may not be enriched with any substantive clinical value as highlighted above. I will therefore refer to this as being the '*non-value*' reasons by default;

'*NON-VALUE*' REASONS WHY GPS MAY SEE REPRESENTATIVES

- Because they 'feel guilty' to refuse access to representatives who have made time to specifically travel to their clinics
- Because they sympathise with representatives whom they perceive to have a difficult job in general
- As a 'sociable' break, away from the stresses of seeing difficult patients during a morning surgery.

The second set of reasons may appear peculiar, but I have heard them given countless times over the years from GPs themselves. And whilst many pharmaceutical managers will probably want to believe that doctors *always* see their representatives because they value the representatives' contributions to the clinical input of patient care, the reality is that this is not always the case.

As I will go on to discuss in chapter 14 the primary aims of a medical representative are to *gain access* to key customers, and to *influence their prescribing.* The crux of this chapter is to point out to readers that the third challenge which invariably sits in between these two objectives will be the inevitable need to hold clinicians' attention in a way which allows an effective selling interaction to take place. Unfortunately there are too many representatives out there who are 'contact-rate driven', and therefore do not seem to appreciate that getting in front of customers is only the tip of the iceberg in terms of influencing prescribing.

Therefore looking at the two lists above, one can deduce that it may be much easier to engage in a more serious dialogue with the type of GP who is motivated by the *first* set of reasons ('value-reasons'). Those GPs who are motivated to see representatives due to the *second* set of reasons, will arguably NOT rank sales discussions as having too high importance once they have simply agreed to see you. You will therefore find that many of these GPs may not form the captive audience that you will need in order to be able to influence prescribing.

Above, we have looked at why some doctors *do* choose to accommodate representative visits. It is now worth looking at the alternate group of doctors who choose *not* to see medical representatives.

In my own experience I strongly believe that the reasons for *NOT* seeing representatives will fall broadly into one of the three categories which I propose below. It is also worth noting that whilst the lists which I gave above were fairly random, the following list is *deliberately* ranked, and can therefore be viewed as a continuum of reasons why doctors choose *not* to see representatives;

REASONS WHY DOCTORS *DO NOT* SEE REPRESENTATIVES

1. They are resolutely opposed to being influenced by pharmaceutical salespeople and have therefore *never* entertained the idea of seeing representatives.
2. They previously used to see representatives, but have since had a bad experience with one or two of them, so have chosen not to see any more at all. Alternatively, they possibly used to see reps but now feel they have no time to be able to afford them, in light of their increased workloads.
3. They have rarely or never seen representatives simply because they have never really perceived any great value in doing so. They *do not* however, take any great issue against the industry, but because they are perceived by most local representatives as being 'no-see' GPs, many reps will not have even tried to access them.

As I stated at the start of this chapter much of a medical representative's energy is invariably spent on trying to see the type of hard access customers listed above. This is because of the stretching coverage targets which tend to be associated with GP target lists (also see chapter 18). Ultimately, the reason this situation occurs is that pharma companies will always incentivise their sales representatives to try and access the highest value customers. Unfortunately in reality, customer profiling is usually based on prescription potential alone, and rarely takes into account the accessibility of a customer. If therefore, your target list throws up a cluster of prescribers who do not routinely see representatives, then you will *still* have the arduous task of having to *try* and access them.

Therefore when looking at the list of reasons as to why these GPs choose *not* to entertain representative visits, it poses an interesting question: *Which one of these customer groups will you be most likely to see (if any)? Which ones are most likely to be receptive to you?*

I would tentatively suggest that the first set of customers (no.1's) will be very set in their thinking and will probably stand by their convictions. I have tried accessing these customers in the past and whilst I may have been lucky to have had one-off visits with a handful of these customers, I would say that overall it is near impossible to maintain any type of productive frequency with them.

The second group of customers will again be difficult to crack because they have either been 'stung' by a previous representative interaction (e.g. a representative may have been too forceful, or may have upset or offended the GP in some other way). Otherwise, these GPs may simply have lost interest in seeing representatives altogether. I believe that these customers will *not* be *impossible* to access, since they did at one time perceive *some* value in seeing representatives. They will however, still be difficult to see.

The final set of customers however (those who have until now, *not perceived* any value in seeing representatives), are the ones who I believe are the 'untapped goldmines'. This is because I have consistently found that these customers (many of whom I *have* managed to get in front of over the years) tend to be quite liberal in their views about your competitive arguments, and are very often more willing to take note of your points – much more so than those customers who see a number of representative details week-in week-out. Therefore to coin a phrase which I used above, you will often find that this audience is *highly* captive – firstly because they have very little prior knowledge of your product, and secondly because they will have rarely heard a structured product detail in quite the way which you are trained to deliver – i.e. their only previous way of finding out about products will have been by laboriously reading about them in medical texts such as the Monthly Index of Medical Specialities (MIMS), or the British National Formulary (BNF).

Therefore if through your professionalism, skill and perseverance you *can* convince these doctors to see you, you could uncover a whole new set of prescribers who have previously been untouched.

As I have said - the reason why I have felt it important to explore this whole subject in detail is that many GPs who appear on representative target lists these days *do* tend to be hard to access, or complete 'no-see' customers. Therefore this issue is extremely prevalent and one which will no doubt need to be tackled as soon as you start working on your target list once you *are* out in the field.

I would therefore advise that if you are faced with such a situation when working through your target list, then you should do some research to find out who potentially, could be those untapped 'category-3 GPs'. This can quite easily be done by speaking to practice staff to try and build a picture of what previous interactions (if any) a GP may have had with representatives. Just by asking them the simple question of WHY it is that their GP does not see representatives could yield the necessary answer to this question.

In summary you will see that much before the skill of selling is applied within this job, the issue of access really does need to be addressed by medical representatives. Therefore knowing *how* to access your key customers –

and in fact *which* key customers to access, should be regarded as very much of a skill within itself!

6. NHS FOCUS: PRIMARY CARE TRUSTS (PCTs)

Throughout this book reference is made to the term 'primary care'. To explain to readers what is meant by primary care, the term refers to the medical services offered to you when you first have a health problem. For this reason primary care usually refers to care offered by General Practitioners (GPs). Unless a patient had a life threatening emergency, they would in the first instance, be offered care by their community GP – hence the name *primary* care is most closely associated with GP practices. Those patients whose condition either cannot be managed by a GP, those who need extra testing, or even those who may need a second opinion, are then referred on to a hospital – hence the term *secondary care* is most closely associated with hospitals and hospital trusts.

Primary Care Trusts (or PCTs) are local NHS organisations which have been set up around the country to fund, plan and provide health services for residents within specified geographical boundaries. These powers and responsibilities have previously been held with the Department Of Health through local health authorities, but have slowly been devolved down to the level of PCTs, which is why these mini-organisations have become so important. It is therefore relevant to acknowledge the existence of Primary Care Trusts (PCTs) as a whole, since primary *and* secondary care services (i.e. services offered by GPs *and* hospitals) are operational within geographical PCTs.

PCTs have tended to have been aligned to local boroughs which are geographically distinct not only for the purposes of medical care, but for all social and environmental services such as housing and education. You will find that as a medical representative, you will most likely cover a number of GP practices which fall across multiple PCTs.

In terms of personnel, PCTs have traditionally been made up of a number of managers for the varying services which have been provided under the banner of medical care. This has tended to take the form of Professional Executive Committees (or 'PECs'). PEC committees have broadly been responsible for setting various policies for PCTs to serve local patient needs. This will have often resulted in them being responsible for controlling local investment and commissioning.

Although PEC committees have constituted a range of managers, they have predominantly been made up of healthcare professionals (such as pharmacists, nurses and GPs). The PEC will also have included the chief executive of the PCT itself. In order for the PECs to have met their clinical objectives for their PCTs, many of them formed sub-committees for the various areas of need. Often, there will have been a bespoke sub-committee for the specific purpose of controlling drug prescribing. This will usually have been in the form of a team of prescribing advisers and prescribing committee members. (These roles are outlined in chapter 16).

As I will go on to discuss, the methods by which PCTs have previously controlled, and are *currently* controlling drug prescribing will vary in their effectiveness. However, because such systems *are* actively in place the activities of PCTs are inevitably a major consideration for pharmaceutical companies who are launching and promoting their medicines directly into these geographical organisations.

It is therefore important to appreciate from the outset, both the current definitions of PCTs and the influence which they have been able to exert on drug prescribing.

As with so many NHS organisations in the past and present however, the size, structure and responsibilities of PCTs as they currently operate are the subject of some debate at the time of this book going to print. Speculation suggests that their very existence may be under threat, or at least they may be subject to some form of restructure or realignment in the near future.

Whatever the outcome of this speculation is however, there are some fundamental principles which I believe will still remain true – they are;

- The NHS will always need some form of prescribing regulation through local management or advisory bodies
- This will invariably involve input by clinical as well as non-clinical managers
- Finally, I believe that GPs will always be answerable to some system which monitors their prescribing habits, which means that autonomous prescribing will still never be as prevalent as it has been in the past.

It is my belief therefore, that whatever format the imminent restructure will take, the principles for prescribing influence and control which are outlined in this book will still be applicable. Therefore, prescribing influence which is exerted by the pharmaceutical industry will still need to be a multifaceted task which will involve influence of both high level advisers, as well as local/end stage clinicians (i.e. GPs).

7. NHS FOCUS; BRANDS Vs. GENERICS AND THE COST OF MEDICINES

Drug spend is recognised as being a major source of expenditure faced by the NHS. In the year to September 2005 (in general practice alone), the number of prescription items issued was in excess of 700million, and the *cost* of these items exceeded a staggering £7.7bn[2]. Therefore in a massive national project to try and save the NHS money, clinicians in recent years have been encouraged and even *incentivised* to prescribe all medications generically. The reason for this is that whilst generic preparations are identical to the branded equivalents in therapeutic effect, they are significantly cheaper in price.

Traditionally in pharmaceuticals, a company will develop drugs for use in various diseases and conditions. From inception, a name will be given to the unique ingredient contained within the product - this is called the *generic* name of the drug (also known as International Non-proprietary Name, or 'INN'). When the company eventually launches the drug to market they will have developed a brand name which is then attached to this generic name. Therefore each drug on the market will be recognised by both a *generic* and a *brand* name.

Brand names have finite legal patents, and only the company who produces the original molecule are allowed to produce and market that product until the initial patent expires. The length of a patent is usually 8-10 years, though the exact length will vary according to how quickly a company is able to launch a drug after a clinical license has been obtained.

---

[2] *'Update on growth in prescription volume and cost year to September 2005'* Prescription Pricing Authority January 2006: www.ppa.org.uk

At the end of this patent life, the drug is then legally able to be reproduced by other companies with the exact active ingredients kept unchanged (these will usually be done by companies who specialise in generic medications – they are often referred to as 'generic houses'). As stated, a generic drug will invariably be considerably cheaper than its branded equivalent and this is ultimately why the NHS are encouraging all drugs to be prescribed generically.

So what happens if a drug patent has *not* expired? Well a doctor can still prescribe a drug by its brand *or* its generic name, but only the *branded* version will be available. Therefore the cost of this drug will be the same whether it is prescribed by brand *or* by its generic name.

Despite this, the Department of Health believe that if all drugs are prescribed generically from the outset then those patients who are on long term repeat medications will automatically be switched over to the less costly generic versions once the drug patents run out. The reason for this is that pharmacists enjoy greater profit margins on generic medicines, and so they will inevitably stock these items in once they become available. Therefore without a doctor having to make any change to a prescription, he will automatically benefit from a significant price decrease in his patient's cost of treatment.

If however, a doctor continues to prescribe a drug by its brand name then the more expensive version will be dispensed – to the financial detriment of the doctor, the PCT, the Strategic Health Authority (StHA), the Department of Health and ultimately to the NHS itself as a whole. Therefore, the 'strategy' of the Department of Health is to revert doctors to habitually naming *all* drugs on prescriptions by their *generic* name, so that when product patents eventually *do* expire, a huge movement in prescribing logistics will not be required by *doctors* (because as stated, this upheaval will invariably be effected by pharmacists).

As a matter of interest, it should also be noted that hospitals are now only able to accept in-patient prescriptions which are written generically. This is why you will find that all hospital physicians will almost exclusively address drugs by their generic names.

Looking at how this money struggle takes shape, it becomes clear why so many major drug companies (through their market leading brands) have quite literally suffered the loss of tens of millions of pounds worth of revenue overnight. As the old saying goes, *'one man's loss is another man's gain'*, and in this case the loss to the pharmaceutical industry really does directly become the gain of the NHS.

Apart from enriching readers with the general background knowledge surrounding this issue, it is also worth noting an important action point to take away from this chapter, which encompasses another major consideration to add into the issue of brand vs. generic prescribing. This particular suggestion surrounds the need to balance the promotion of a branded drug against the need to be customer focussed in how you promote your products.

What I mean by this is that pharmaceutical companies will invariably develop specific and targeted advertising campaigns which centre around the *brand* name of a drug. Therefore in order for clinicians to be able to associate particular advertising campaigns with individual drugs, companies obviously want their representatives to promote their drugs by brand name. However as discussed above, because clinicians are now prescribing all drugs generically they will obviously have to remember the *generic* name of your drug if they intend to actually prescribe it.

My solution to this problem therefore, is to simply promote all drugs by both *brand,* and by generic name - almost within the same breath! Therefore each and every time you verbally mention the brand name, you should always ensure that it is closely associated with the generic name too. This serves two major needs:

1. From a *marketing perspective,* your products are identified with advertising campaigns and therefore linked into carefully developed 'brand values' (this is also discussed in chapter 13)
2. From a *prescriber's perspective* you are also fulfilling an inherent need – which is to ensure that they are reminded about *exactly* what they will have to issue on a prescription if they intend to prescribe your drug.

I have used this technique for years, and whilst it may sound confusing and fussy in print, I can assure readers that it becomes much clearer once you are out on territory, promoting your products to prescribers.

8. NHS FOCUS; THE GREAT STRUGGLE BETWEEN PHARMACEUTICAL PROSPERITY AND NHS FUNDING

For the purpose of this text I shall only attempt to cover this debate in its basic form, since it could quite easily become a book within itself!

As I mentioned above, the NHS *must* (as part of their national plans for health improvement), set aside funding for drug prescribing since prescription drugs constitute such a significant cost to the NHS.

Drugs of course, are developed by private sector pharmaceutical companies, whereas the NHS (as a public sector organisation) only have limited funds available to be able to 'pay' for these medicines. Despite the introduction of drug formularies (discussed in chapter 10) doctors have still been able to exercise autonomy in their prescribing which has meant that they have been able to prescribe even the most expensive medications if they feel there is a genuine medical need to do so.

So here is the battle! Pharmaceutical companies can only fund the future research of new drugs by the money they earn *today* (which effectively, is just like any other business). Therefore the way in which pharmaceutical companies fund their existence and prosperity, is by maximising the revenues from promoting the medicines which they *currently* have available on the market.

The flipside of the argument is that those doctors who prescribe more expensive medications effectively bind the NHS to pay for these medicines (because the NHS currently has little power to be able to change the initial choice of drug which is prescribed by a doctor) – regardless of how expensive it is. Therefore many NHS managers, (and even many medical practitioners) believe that the commercial activities of pharmaceutical companies (*although completely legal – as deemed by the ABPI*) can put an unnecessary strain on NHS funding. So ultimately, the conflict which exists is borne out of the need for pharma companies to balance the costs of today, with managing existence for tomorrow.

The pharmaceutical industry rightly believe that they should be credited with many of the ground breaking medicinal developments seen over the past century. It could be argued that the longer life expectancy and ageing of the UK population is clear evidence of this success (due to the fact that many modern drugs have specifically been developed to contain diseases and conditions in patients of *all* ages to a point where overall survival has improved).

Even if this debate is considered purely on cost terms then many would say that innovative, safe and effective medications (although costly themselves) can actually save the NHS vast amounts of money and resource in the long term through the prevention of otherwise having to manage uncontrolled illnesses as they become progressively worse. By this we mean the potential costs of patient hospitalisation, the possible need for surgical interventions and the overall care that would need to be administered to patients who may then be too far progressed in their illnesses to be managed by drugs alone. Considering financial costs in such holistic terms is a concept known as health economics.

Therefore many opinion leaders within the pharmaceutical industry believe that although the government perceive that they are effectively managing NHS costs through control mechanisms such as drug formularies, such measures are arguably short-termist tactics, because if pharmaceutical companies' profits are not able to flourish due to obstructions from prescribing authorities today, then their research and drug developments of tomorrow will suffer, and ultimately the government will have to manage illnesses through other resources (mentioned above) which themselves are *already* under strain.

Some would say that this argument is almost as simple as being *'proactive'* Vs. *'reactive'*. It could be said that the *proactive* use of effective medicines *now,* will avoid the need to *reactively* deal with spiralling costs in other areas *later.*

Once again, I must clearly state that this is just *one* viewpoint of this debate, and by no means representative of all the issues that prevail – (it *should* nonetheless give you a simple snapshot of the key issues within this conflict).

So what does this mean for the price of medicines? Well each doctor/practice is allocated a set budget which is dedicated to drug spend – so although doctors do not actually pay for medicines themselves, they *are* nonetheless accountable for how they manage their allocated budget. Therefore when a doctor complains that they feel a drug is 'too expensive', they will be referring to the strain which this puts on their *allocated budget,* and not directly on their bank accounts (of course!) Ultimately though, doctors *will* be answerable to their PCTs as to why they have overspent on their budget allocations so this *is* a very real concern for them.

This budget monitoring however, presents issues within itself. As some of the more opinionated doctors have commented in the past, *"If the NHS/ PCTs are going to block us from using particular medications, then why do the authorities grant these drugs licenses in the first place?"* (In reality of course, it is the Medicines and Healthcare products Regulatory Agency (MHRA) who actually grant products their licenses).

The reason why this conflict exists however, is down to something which I believe is so often seen in business and politics, and quite simply boils down to *size, sophistication and accountability.* What I mean by this is that because the NHS as an organisation is itself so vast, each stakeholder-group within it (and even peripherally), is responsible for just a small part of the bigger picture. In this case, the scope of the MHRA is simply to assess if they believe a medicine has sufficient clinical data to back up a clinical license which has been applied for.

As for how the medicine producer (pharmaceutical company) *then* decides to price the drug, is very much based on their own discretion and therefore has nothing to do with the MHRA within their scope of influence.

So when a pharmaceutical company sets the price for a drug they will usually determine this by commercial considerations such as the price of competitor products in the same class/therapy area, and by how much it has cost the company to bring this product to market, (and therefore how quickly the company projects that the drugs sales can return a profit).

In this way, the MHRA effectively leaves it to institutions such as the National Institute for Health and Clinical Excellence (NICE), Strategic Health Authorities and PCTs to approve and 'police' the use of medicines with *monetary* as well as *clinical* considerations in mind. Therefore one may argue that the interests of the MHRA are broadly clinical, the interests of the NHS are financial *containment* and clinical *attainment,* and the interests of pharmaceutical companies lie in financial returns on investments – hence the inevitable struggle which ensues between such closely linked, yet aspirationally diverse stakeholders.

(The role of NICE is summarised in chapter 16).

9. NHS FOCUS: THE CHANGING ENVIRONMENT OF GENERAL PRACTICE

As I have already alluded to in chapter 6, the backdrop in which GPs carry out their work changes so rapidly, that it is extremely tempting *not to* write about the 'current' issues which are affecting GPs. It is difficult however, to ignore the impact which phenomena such as the new GP Contract has had on the way doctors practice in this country. Again, it is worth remembering that this subject could quite feasibly fill a text book in its own right, but for the benefit of my readers I will once again try and cover this topic in its basic form.

Over the years there have been numerous changes which have influenced the way general practice operates – GP fundholding, Primary Care Groups (PCGs), Primary Care Trusts (PCTs) and National Service Frameworks (NSFs) to name just a few.

Modern UK governments have consistently placed public health as a priority under their political manifestos and improvement plans. As part of this vision, the NHS confederation (representing the four UK governments) has worked with the British Medical Association (BMA) to develop a new GP contract (known as the new General Medical Services, or 'New GMS Contract'). This contract was designed to improve the working conditions of GPs, to reward practices for achieving quality in pre-specified patient outcomes, and ultimately therefore to offer a better quality of care to patients.

Just to give readers a background, GPs have previously operated as independent contractors to the NHS where they have offered standards of care to patients which *they* believe are best, based on the most up to date best practice in medicine. Therefore, the level of care which they have offered has ultimately been based on *their own* individual skill and discretion as medical practitioners. The way GPs have been remunerated *before* the new contract therefore, is that they have been paid primarily based on *how many patients* they are responsible for on their practice list, rather than what standard of care they have achieved for these patients (a system known as capitation payments). This has been seen to have caused an inconsistency in the standard of care which has been provided by GP practices nationally.

The most notable outcome from the new GMS contract has been the formation of a clear, unambiguous set of clinical and organisational targets – the Quality and Outcomes Framework, or 'QOF'. This has meant that every GMS practice in the country must now work towards a consistent set of standards for quality and most notably, they will have been paid according to how well they have performed against these common standards, as opposed to how many patients they serve. In brief, each quality point achieved in the financial year 2005/6 was worth an average of £120.00 to a practice, with a maximum of 1050 points available overall. In 2006, there were further points allocated which included recognition of an increased number of clinical areas, and acknowledgement of the Practice Based Commissioning initiative in England.

This change in remuneration has resulted in GPs being incentivised to work in quite a different way to that which they have previously been used to. Naturally (as with *any* major industrial change) the new contract has therefore been met with various responses from primary care practitioners which range from apathy, resistance, frustration, right up to those clinicians who really have embraced the opportunity which the new contract has presented them with. Practices are now having to work collaboratively as organisational teams to cover all the quality areas and in doing so, are very often at full stretch much of the time!

Due to this inevitable increase in workload, the new contract is *yet another* factor which has made medical representative access to GPs more difficult. Despite this, the new contract has also created a huge window of opportunity for the pharmaceutical industry, because those companies who have developed value added services *and* who have promoted their medicines in a way which recognises and complements the new contract, have clearly been in a stronger position to be able to forge more meaningful relationships with their key practices.

Of course, no company can *expect* to have their products more favourably prescribed if they support practices in this way (such conduct is strictly against ABPI guidelines), but clearly those companies who *can, and have* demonstrated to their customers that they recognise the constraints which have been placed on them, will be perceived by customers as being more serious, professional organisations. Using and developing such working relationships really has allowed the more conscientious representatives and companies to prove their worth as professional partners to GP practices – almost in a way of 'natural selection' from those who have *not* been so wise as to recognise this change to the customer environment.

Such is the opportunity, that there are now a number of independent organisations who specialise in developing programmes which meet the needs of both NHS customers and of those pharmaceutical companies who wish to use such programmes. One such organisation is Axis Development – a company whose vision and aim is to be the interface between the pharmaceutical industry and the NHS[3]. They offer a wide range of programmes for

---

[3] Axis Development: www.axis-development.co.uk

Continuing Professional Development (CPD) which allows both the pharmaceutical industry *and* the NHS to build mutually beneficial relationships.

The New GP Contract has provided both an interesting and challenging climate in which GPs are now practising, and this subject will undoubtedly be one of the most visible which representatives will observe in primary care for the foreseeable future.

The bottom line for new representatives is: learn this chapter, know the basic issues and what they mean to customers, learn the exact requirements which customers must demonstrate in those therapy areas in which you are promoting, and do not underestimate the impact that this new contract is having on the way in which you will have to work with your customers.

PRACTICE BASED COMMISSIONING – THE NEXT BIG CHANGE AFTER THE NEW CONTRACT

In much the same way as the new GMS contract has swept across the NHS and influenced the way primary care services are offered, Practice Based Commissioning, or 'PBC' is without doubt the next major NHS initiative which will impact on General Practice (in England).

As a top-line explanation, Practice Based Commissioning is a concept whereby practices will hold budgets, and take accountability for the organisation and costs associated with providing certain local medical services. The aim is for practices to be responsible for offering a better *quality* of service to their patients, and in doing so, to free up money to be able to redirect to *other local* services.

Therefore in implementing Practice Based Commissioning, practices and localities will be empowered to determine *which* services are available to their patients, in addition to determining the *range* and *quality* of these services – in line with local needs. In this way, practices will invariably take more ownership and accountability of how much impact these services have on local PCT expenditure.

Currently, in offering medical care to their patients, practices utilise various NHS resources such as;

- Drugs
- Diagnostic resources (such as heart, blood, ultrasound, X-ray and other monitoring)
- 'Scheduled care' (such as surgical operations)
- And 'unscheduled care' (such as emergency patient referrals).

In fact, the Department Of Health have highlighted practices as being the main determinants of health care utilisation overall [4] . The problem however, is that currently, practices only receive 'feedback' on how much resource they are using up in the form of prescribing. This is mainly done via Prescribing Analysis and CosT (or PACT) data.

PACT data basically gives (quarterly) statistical breakdowns of how a practice has performed on various prescribing measures, such as their periodic drug spend versus local and national averages. This tool tends to be used for planning and really, just to allow GP practices to track how their prescribing habits are changing over a given period of time.

As stated – apart from this, practices are not really given any indication as to how much resource they are using in

---

[4] *'Practice Based Commissioning: Engaging Practices in Commissioning'* Department Of Health, 5/10/2004: www.dh.gov.uk

the other mentioned areas, and therefore what impact this is having on costs and capacity within a wider geographical network (such as a PCT). Also, because these resources are regarded by the practice as being 'external', practices are not able to influence the level of quality of these services.

Therefore the idea of PBC is that practices will work towards developing and delivering a plan for extra services to be able to meet the exact medical needs of *their* local patients. These plans and provisions may be organised on an individual practice basis, or even as a group of locality practices. Again, the beauty of the system is that either format is allowable and applicable, and is based purely on local need as and how they are perceived to be required by practices themselves.

The PCT would then release funds (in the format of something called an 'indicative budget') in order for these services to be realised. As it is envisaged that commissioning services in this way will free up money due to more efficient working, it has then been agreed that this extra/freed up money can then be redirected and used either to improve *other* patient services, or to pay practices for the inevitable management costs associated with creating such services. (It is actually the PCT's PEC Committee who is set to ensure that this extra money is being used appropriately).

The government envisage that patients will benefit from PBC in the following ways:

- Patients may be offered a greater *variety* of services
- There may be more people/centres offering these services (therefore *greater access* and availability)
- Such centres may be more (geographically) local to patients than they were previously

In addition, the government also believe that the NHS itself will benefit from PBC due to more efficient use of resources, and from greater involvement of front line doctors and nurses. Another benefit could be that practices may well be able to commission services that previously were not available, such as specialist nurses for example.

So what impact will Practice Based Commissioning have on you as a medical representative? What opportunities will this present for the pharmaceutical industry? In reality, the exact impact which it will have is difficult to predict because at the time of this book going to print, Practice Based Commissioning is a concept which is still very much in its infancy. Another reason why it is difficult to predict its effects, is that the whole basis of the concept is that funds will be directed towards *individual* local needs. Therefore it would not be unreasonable to suggest that its impact could look vastly different as you travel from one *area to the next,* or even from one *practice* to the next.

What I *would* put my money on, is that there will undoubtedly be *further* time constraints on GPs since in effect, they will be monitoring quality achievements within their practices (as required by the Quality and Outcomes Framework of the GMS contract), whilst *also* having to find time to monitor and manage progress towards PBC initiatives.

In terms of opportunities, it would seem that GPs will have a greater potential to initiate medicines since (for example) diagnostic referrals could benefit from far quicker turnaround times, therefore allowing GPs to make quicker decisions about treatment needs. Also, expert clinicians (such as consultants or GPs with special expertise) may well run extra clinics to serve local needs, which again, will result in quicker referral turnaround time and increased GP prescribing from the subsequent clinical recommendations made during these specialist consultations.

Apart from these possible effects on prescribing, I can only speculate that in terms of opportunities for the pharmaceutical industry to support practices in PBC implementation, there may be some potential in areas of clinical and organisational need such as:

- IT/software solutions which analyse the flow and utilisation of commissioned monies
- Training programmes for individuals or practices in areas such as negotiation skills, or effective team working
- Training programmes for *entire localities* based on the above subjects
- Training programmes aimed at improving actual commissioning skills

In principle, Practice Based Commissioning has been available to be utilised from April 2005 onwards, but unlike the impact of the new contract which was almost universally inclusive, I believe that only the most proactive practices, localities and PCTs will *immediately* respond to the opportunity of the PBC initiative. Until then, I envisage that its impact will still be overshadowed by GPs adjustment to managing the long term requirements of the new GMS contract, but DO be prepared for when it DOES take effect!

10. THE IMPACT OF FORMULARIES IN PRIMARY CARE

As the local sales representative for your product, you will need to find out if local prescribing authorities have endorsed the use of your product, or even if they have applied any formal restrictions to its use. If such directives *have* been issued, they will most likely be in the form of drug formularies or guidelines which specifically recommend the use of either yours, or a competitor's product.

Formularies are prescribing guidance documents which are produced by groups of clinicians (sometimes with the aid of NHS managers) in order to help them to exercise a level of control and uniformity of prescribing amongst the constituents of a particular institution – usually a GP practice, a hospital or an entire Primary Care Trust (these are the three stakeholder groups who most commonly use drug formularies).

PCT FORMULARIES

PCT formularies offer complete prescribing guidance to constituent primary care clinicians, and will often aim to limit the number of drugs which can be used within a particular class or 'family' of drug. Their level of enforcement varies from "guidance/reference only" right up to a direct recommendation. The reasons that PCTs will want GPs to adhere to their guidance can vary, but may be due to the following;

- PCTs may budget for the cost of the recommended drug, therefore wide scale use of *alternative* drugs may result in a PCT exceeding their drug spend (especially if these alternative products are more expensive)

- PCTs may believe that there is a certain amount of risk involved in using drugs which are relatively new and untested, and they will therefore use formularies to recommend the use of tried and tested therapies
- Finally, and perhaps most interestingly, PCTs *themselves* are actually measured and appraised on the level of formulary adherence which their constituent GPs will demonstrate. This will be monitored by Strategic health Authorities (StHAs)

A GPs failure to comply with *strict* formulary recommendations can result in them (or their practice) having to explain to the PCT *why* they have gone against the local guidance which everyone has been expected to follow. Interestingly though, other than scrutinising individual GP practices through such prescribing discussions, a PCT can not actually do a great deal more to *disincentivise* a GP from prescribing a drug 'off-formulary'.

In my own experience however, if doctors are aware of their PCT's expectations of them, this is very often enough to dissuade them from deliberately prescribing against such recommendations. As one of my customers once said, *"we are well aware that technically, PCTs cannot do a great deal to stop us from prescribing against local recommendations. There is however an unspoken understanding amongst experienced GPs that we should stick to what they recommend. This is because when it comes to us needing to approach them for support in other areas they may well decide to use discretion in how they allocate resource and support. So although such a hypothesis is not proven, many of us nonetheless believe that it is prudent to stay on the good side of your PCT – as this is for our own ultimate interests".*

As with any situation however, there will always be some slightly more opinionated (and some would say 'rebellious') prescribers who will be damned if they are to be told *what*, and what *not* to prescribe! The key point to remember is that (perhaps controversially), autonomous prescribing *can* and still *does* occur quite regularly within the NHS. One of the key aims of a medical representative therefore, should be to seek to understand the extent to which prescribers actually adhere to guidance as this can vary dramatically from one institution to the next.

Other forms of prescribing guidance derived from formularies are prescribing guidelines, prescribing protocols, or clinical management plans. These terms are fairly interchangeable, but a key difference from formularies is that the latter two variations will usually focus on one particular disease or class of drug, rather than general drug formularies which tend to encompass *all* clinical areas of prescribing.

A prescribing guideline may be issued to supplement a formulary *if* for example, a drug has gained a new license, or if a completely new drug has been launched. This would save the PCT from having to re-write an entire formulary. Another situation where a guideline may be used, is if there are specific considerations which need to be addressed if a specialist drug is to be prescribed a particular way.

Protocols and clinical management plans tend to give more direction as to how *exactly* a drug should be used. Protocols are popular where a 'shared-care' approach to using a drug may be appropriate. For example, a hospital may need to initiate a particular drug which then needs to be monitored in a specific way by primary care practitioners. In such a scenario, a protocol may then be expressed as a flow diagram which gives guidance on what courses of action to take as a patient progresses through various stages of an illness or condition.

In the above way, you can probably see that formularies, guidelines, protocols and clinical management plans can be your greatest friend *or* foe! That is, if your drugs *are* included on them, you can expect local advisers to automatically endorse their use, and at the same time ensure that competitor products are not used. Conversely, the disadvantages of not being included on a local formulary are also clear to see.

The responsibility of driving your product onto PCT guidelines will be the responsibility of your Healthcare Development Manager (HDM). It is their job to sell your product benefits to influencers at PCT level, although some of these influencers may have dual roles as GPs *and* as PCT executives (also see chapter 16). This will mean that both you *and* your HDM will have a requirement to see these particular customers.

A final issue to consider under PCT formulary development is the need to determine which factors actually influence PCT formulary inclusions. It is fair to say that most often, the key considerations tend to be those of cost and clinical evidence. As for which one of these factors is predominant, will vary significantly from one trust to the next. As stated, within pharmaceutical organisations, it is the responsibility of the HDM to present such information to prescribing managers at PCT level, though these managers may in turn seek to establish such data from hospital physicians (particularly in the case of clinical evidence).

But even though cost and drug evidence tend to be the foremost influencing factors for PCT formulary development, it has also been known for primary care practitioners to *upwardly influence* PCT formulary development. How is this? Well as mentioned above, PCTs are partly measured on the level of formulary adherence which they can demonstrate. Therefore when deciding which drugs to include on a formulary a PCT may simply look at which product is most commonly prescribed within their locality – the idea being that if one particular drug is known to be popular amongst the majority of constituent prescribers, then endorsing this as the choice product in class will automatically result in greater formulary adherence.

HOSPITAL FORMULARIES

Hospitals also use formularies, though theirs are used to exercise control on what is prescribed *within* hospitals. In this way PCTs are theoretically able to retain some control of what is recommended to their GPs. As stated, despite the fact that hospital formularies are commissioned for secondary care prescribing, they are well known to directly influence primary care prescribing too. This is due to two main reasons;

Firstly, if a patient is admitted to hospital for an acute condition then any drugs which the patient is prescribed may need to be administered over the long term to control their condition. Therefore GPs will have to repeat-prescribe whatever has been started by the hospital. An example may be a patient who is admitted to the hospital due to a heart attack. Whilst the hospital will care for this patient for a week or so whilst the patient recovers, it is the *GP* who will then have to continue issuing the various heart medications which have been started at the hospital – in fact, in heart attack cases in particular, the drugs which are started will generally have to be taken by the patient for the rest of their life.

The second way in which hospital formularies influence GP prescribing is that when GPs are making prescribing choices, they will often look to what is being recommended and prescribed at their local hospitals since they trust the clinical judgements of their local professors and consultants. Therefore if a GP had to initiate a drug himself, he may well choose to prescribe those drugs which he has seen being issued recently by the local hospital.

Whilst the above examples highlight the way in which hospital formularies dictate what is prescribed by hospital doctors, this relationship can also be a converse one. What I mean by this is that the choice of drugs which a consultant decides to initiate can also have a huge influence as to what actually *ends up* on the hospital formulary. Vast numbers of drugs that are on hospital formularies today have got there as a result of *consultants* lobbying for their local approval.

In essence this makes perfect sense, since drug formularies need to be dynamic and cyclical in order for new therapies to be accommodated and utilised. Otherwise how would new drugs ever be used? It could also be said that this scenario represents the way in which upward influence can also take effect in a hospital setting – (as was described in PCT formulary development above).

In fact, consultant opinion and influence can often affect what happens at PCT level also, and many trusts take the view that hospital and PCT formularies should be linked for practical reasons relating to formulary adherence – i.e. a GP (who can often be bombarded with advice and influence from a variety of sources as to what to prescribe), is more likely to conform to a prescribing guidance if it has been jointly issued from two locally recognised 'authorities' (a hospital *and* a PCT).

Another reason for the influence of hospitals on PCT formularies is that, (in just the way that *GPs* look towards hospital doctors as being experts in their clinical fields), *prescribing managers* within PCTs (such as prescribing advisers) may also put great faith in the judgement of hospital clinicians since, by virtue of who they are, consultants will often have the most informed and robust knowledge of respective therapy areas. (Prescribing advisers are discussed in chapter 16).

In much the same way as PCT formularies fall within the remit of HDMs, the determination of what is included on the *hospital* formulary is usually the responsibility of your hospital sales representative. However many companies use primary care representatives to influence hospital prescribing as part of their afternoon activities, so this responsibility often becomes integrated (this is also covered in chapter 16).

Looking at the work of pharmaceutical salespeople therefore, it follows that many drug formularies are achieved on the basis of strong collaboration between both the HDM and the hospital representative who will each work to lobby their respective target customers to drive through joint formulary developments.

PRACTICE FORMULARIES

The third and final type of formulary you may encounter in your work is the *practice* formulary. This is more likely to occur in larger (group) practices. The idea here is that all prescribers *within the practice* should stick to an agreed prescribing list – (which is why all practice stakeholders will usually be involved in developing such a formulary). Some practices however, choose to develop practice formularies with input from a pharmaceutical adviser from the PCT. The principles here are the same as for PCT and hospital formularies – i.e. a set number of drugs are 'approved' for use within given therapy areas and all stakeholders are encouraged to initiate only those drugs which are named on the guidance list.

Overall, the following are some of the advantages to PCTs, hospitals *or* practices of having formularies;

- They can save money on drug expenditure if all prescribers adhere to them (since the consistent use of cost effective medications will by default, eliminate the use of more costly alternatives).
- Clinicians within these organisations will become familiar with particular medications if they consistently use the same ones. (This is particularly useful in drug classes which are clinically indistinguishable, yet flooded with choices).
- Formularies encourage 'shared care' if they are developed in conjunction with any, or all of the partnering organisations discussed above.

In contrast, some of the counter arguments against formularies (particularly from the pharmaceutical industry and indeed many prescribers), are that they can be too inflexible, they very often stifle the potential benefits of new therapies (since very few formularies will immediately take on new drugs until a 'probationary period' is seen out). Most of all, many pragmatists believe that the financial benefits gained from effectively controlling prescribing costs via formularies, will simply be consumed by the very costs of enforcing the formularies themselves.

When this argument is considered in context of PCTs especially, it is fair to say that some PCTs constitute *so many* clinicians, that it is quite easy to see how cumbersome and expensive it could be to exercise direct prescribing control over large numbers of prescribers. Nonetheless, formulary influence on primary care prescribing is clearly on the increase, so is a key factor which needs to be understood by medical representatives.

PART 2

UNDERSTANDING YOUR ROLE

11. JOB PURPOSE OF THE MEDICAL SALES PROFESSIONAL

Primarily, the job purpose of the medical representative can be defined as 'taking responsibility for increasing the sales of promoted product(s) within a defined geographical territory'.

Sales in pharmaceuticals will usually be measured by changes in *cash value*, or by changes in *market share*. To explain to readers what is meant by market share, take the following example:

There may be three painkillers on the market. The combined sales of these three drugs represents the *total* market. Each product generates its own proportion of sales in that market, and it is *this* proportion which is referred to as it's 'market share'. Therefore whatever the respective market share is of each product, the total market will always equate to 100%. Therefore many companies will set their representatives the task of growing their product's market share.

Effectively, the job of a medical representative therefore is **'to *directly influence* prescribing behaviour'**. This succinctly describes what we do, since no matter what volume of your product a GP is currently prescribing, we are (without exception) being paid to influence them towards using *more* of our products where clinically feasible.

In the case of a complete non-prescriber, our job is to displace a competitor's stronghold, and to thereby place our product as the preferential choice in its therapeutic class. In the case of an existing prescriber, we are still trying to change their prescribing habit, but this 'change' now takes the form of expanding our product's usage into further patient populations. Therefore as stated, the consistent aim is towards *influencing* prescribing behaviour in one way or another.

From a less commercial point of view, it is important to appreciate that medical representatives also have a pivotal responsibility in monitoring quality issues for their promoted products – namely recognising and reporting adverse drug events for the purpose of safety monitoring.

This is where clinicians may highlight an adverse event (usually a side effect) that has occurred in a patient whilst using your company's product. Once representatives are made aware of such an occurrence, they are legally bound by the ABPI to report the adverse event to their medical information department who will then record details about the nature of the event. Such practice allows potentially life threatening adverse effects to be investigated and managed in a timely fashion. The role which medical representatives play in this type of safety monitoring cannot be emphasised enough, and was subject to particular focus for the 2006 ABPI Code of Practice update.

The actual *job title* of the medical representative can vary, though the basics of the job remain the same. They may be referred to as *Medical Representatives, Territory Business Managers, Territory Sales Managers or even Key Account Managers*. Also, based on experience and sales achievement, there is often promotion within the sales job itself which would typically progress a representative from a trainee, to a full medical representative, then to a *senior* medical representative, and ultimately to a 'principal' or 'executive' medical representative (as described in chapter 1).

This can be quite a lottery in the sense that unless you are launching a new product, you will always 'inherit' a baseline market share which will have been determined by previous salespeople who have worked on that territory. I have experienced both sides of the coin in this respect. I have previously had to take on a territory where my product had a very small market share. I have also worked in a territory where the previous sales team had already achieved such a high market share, that I literally spent my first few months living in the shadow of their success!

The latter was a unique situation, because whilst many people were envious that I had taken over such a successful territory, *I myself* still felt the burden of having to live up to my predecessors good work. This particular time of my career more than any other, really proved to me that primarily, 'people buy people' because at the first mention of my company or drug name, my customers would immediately make the association with my predecessors – a clear demonstration of the fact that before the product, these customers really did 'buy-into' the people who were selling it (this is discussed further in chapter 21).

Another very important lesson which I learnt was that despite many outsiders perceiving that all the hard work had already been done for me, it later became clear where *I also*, had made my own mark on that territory. Whilst my predecessors spent years cultivating *one* set of key customers, I was able to look after these same customers, *and* to additionally develop a whole new cluster of previously untapped customers. This resulted in us winning additional business.

The lesson to learn from this story is that *all* salespeople are individuals with different strengths and capabilities, and because we work with a variety of customers, one should never underestimate the contribution which *any* individual can make to a new sales territory – whatever the local history is.

The last point to mention in this chapter – and one which I shall only touch on, is the very real need to work effectively in sales *teams* – even within the primary care role. This is quite separate from the need to work in *cross-functional* teams (e.g. with hospital representatives, HDMs and others).

In past decades, companies would only employ one representative to work a sales territory – and usually, they would be working a vast geographical area. In the modern era, many products are now commonly promoted by *teams* of representatives (not to mention the fact that primary care territories are now much smaller). What this results in, is that there will often be more than one of you doing the *same* job in the *same* territory with the *same* customers.

You will therefore find that the requirement to work together in sales teams will be paramount to your success. This can be a *key benefit* if you have a strong team, but this can also be a *major disadvantage* if you find yourself working in a dysfunctional team who are (for whatever reasons) not working collaboratively towards common goals. Once again, this is yet another subject which can fill a text book in its own right, so I shall leave it to the management gurus to explain how to get the best out of the 'team' environment.

My purpose for mentioning this topic is simply to make readers aware that you will almost certainly find yourself plunged into a primary care team of some size, so if you are the type of associate who would not work well with different personalities then this may not be the ideal job for you.

12. SELLING Vs. INFORMING

This issue represents an interesting yet easily confused principle which you will probably have to tackle in many of your customer calls. For this reason, it is necessary to establish a fundamental awareness of the differences between both selling and informing.

In *any* selling situation, 'best practice' would naturally constitute some form of information exchange with customers. This exchange would then culminate in a conclusive sales close (as described previously). In pharmaceuticals however, the great dichotomy is that it is all too easy for representatives to 'give' information without receiving a subsequent commitment to 'buy'.

Therefore doctors could quite happily end a sales call once they have received the 'information' which *they* need. It is therefore up to you as the sales professional to take control of your sales calls and ensure that you achieve the following outcomes;

- You do indeed have to give the information which the doctor requires for himself
- You must also be constantly selling the benefits of your product
- Finally, you *must* try and end the call with some form of commitment to prescribe (if and when it is appropriate to do so).

Really, the take home point from this chapter is to be consciously aware of the two reasons why doctor/medical representative sales calls exist. That is;

1. Why will a *doctor* want to see *you*?
2. And what is YOUR purpose for being there?

It is important to understand this because these motivators are fundamentally different. From the list of reasons of why a doctor would choose to see a representative which I proposed in chapter 5, the *most* common reason for why I believe doctors agree to see representatives is for them to be kept up to date with new drug developments.

So despite this constituting the doctor's main 'need' from seeing representatives, I strongly believe that in order to succeed at all in this job, you must never lose sight of why you are there – TO SELL YOUR PRODUCTS! Not only in a way that will '*keep the doctor informed*', but in a way that will ensure that yours is the drug which is preferentially prescribed by that GP.

It is imperative that you are clear about this when going into your customer calls. After all, clinicians themselves will very often be quite clear in *their* minds about what it is they want from a representative sales call. This is why you will so often go into a call with them starting the discussion with statements such as:

- *"I can only spare you two minutes, so please just give me the key points"*
- *"I know all about your product, so please just tell me what is new"*
- *"Please do not belittle your competitors - just tell me what is good about your drug"*
- *"I only want you to talk about one product – not two or three"*

This demonstrates that many customers will have obviously thought about what it is that *they* want from the call. All I am suggesting is that for your own professional benefit, *you too* must be clear about why you are there, and what you need to achieve from a customer call. I know of some representatives who are confident enough to actually verbalise this at the start of a call (e.g. *"Doctor, what I want to achieve by the end of this call is for you to choose 'X' as your first choice drug in it's class"*), and I know of other representatives who feel that this approach is too forceful.

I personally believe either method can work, just so long as the approach is appropriate to *your* natural style of conversation and selling. Even if you choose not to verbalise an objective such as the one above, it is critical that you *focus your mind* on this objective. Otherwise, you will fall into the trap of giving the doctor what *he* wants, without achieving anything for yourself. This would be a wasted sales opportunity.

Most customers are unlikely to admit that they actually *'want to engage in a selling discussion with a medical representative'*, yet the reality is that they are not I, and they *do* know exactly why you are there. I believe however, that this ends up becoming a fair exchange. That is, the doctor will allow you to see him since he would like to be kept updated with product and therapy area knowledge, but at the same time they are aware and accepting of the fact that whilst in the process of informing them, you will invariably be presenting clinical arguments to justify why you want them to preferentially prescribe your drug.

I know of one very experienced representative who was expertly able to engage customers in polite conversation. He would put customers at ease through small talk, yet he always progressed his sales calls with each of his customers by being clear about what *he* wanted to achieve by the *end* of the call. It was ironic, because whilst he would appear to be an extremely amiable chap to his customers, he would always say to fellow sales professionals that he certainly didn't sit around in GP surgeries just to 'exchange pleasantries!' – his one and only aim would always be to get them to prescribe his product. Some may say this approach was a little aggressive, but it certainly was successful for him.

I will go on to summarise my recommendations around sales closing in my 7th Golden Principle of Success in chapter 21.

13. WHAT MAKES A DOCTOR PRESCRIBE A PRODUCT?

The question of what makes a doctor choose a product is fundamentally the 'million dollar question!' The list of variables is huge, and arguably there will never be a way of determining what *exactly* changes prescribing behaviour. It is also fair to say that whatever it is that *does* make doctors choose a drug will vary from one prescriber to the next. I once heard a top sales representative suggest that "*Doctors tend to have a key reason why they choose to prescribe drugs. Our job is simply to find this key and unlock it*".

Imagine yourself as a consumer looking to purchase new double glazing for example. In order to influence which glazing product you choose, competing companies will spend huge amounts of time, money and resource in trying to influence your eventual choice through sales reps, billboard adverts, leaflets in magazines, telesales, television advertising etc. The lists are sometimes endless depending on which products we are dealing with.

In much the same way, pharmaceutical companies will also try their best to affect the vast range of mediums/methods for influencing 'purchasing' (or prescribing) behaviour in medicines.

In the case of pharmaceuticals, the key factors which are thought to influence prescribing behaviour include the following (in no particular order);

- Adverts in the medical press
- Direct mailings
- Opinions of local consultants and professors (which may be expressed through drug formularies)
- Opinions of local prescribing advisers (which again, may be expressed through formularies)

- National 'opinion-leader' endorsements (i.e. expert clinicians specialising in particular therapy areas)
- Expert medical society opinions (such as the British Hypertension Society, the British Thoracic Society, the British Association of Dermatology etc)
- 'NICE' endorsements
- Spontaneous recall (i.e. what they remember!)
- Clinical evidence
- Patient influence
- The price of a drug
- Competitive pricing deals offered to dispensing practices
- The clinicians own past experience of a drug in their own patients
- Finally of course, visits from medical sales representatives themselves.

Some pharmaceutical marketers even believe that the 'brand characteristics' of a product may have a part to play in influencing a product's uptake i.e. what are the non-clinical aspects of a product which determine how it is perceived by clinicians – e.g. is it perceived as modern, cutting edge and innovative? Or is it simply seen as uninteresting, old or perhaps even just a 'me-too' product?

As discussed, the list of possible influences is vast, and the precise extent to which each, *or* any one of these factors actually affects a prescribers choice are infinitely debatable. One thing is for certain however, that the majority of pharmaceutical companies will invariably try to influence as many of these mediums as possible in an attempt to maximise product success. Any company that chooses to neglect *any* of the listed influences would be doing so at their own commercial risk.

The major point which *is* very much agreed upon, is the impact which pharmaceutical sales representatives have on prescribing. The formula is apparently simple –

employ a sales force to sell your product 'live' to prescribers, and that product's sales will invariably increase. There seems to be no better way to reach out and directly influence a prescriber, than to be sold to by a pharmaceutical sales professional. This basic principle has kept alive the existence and indeed the growth of medical sales representatives, literally for decades. It is from here therefore, that I propose my theory on the *'GP circle of influence'* and how this is likely to affect GP prescribing.

14. ACCOUNT MANAGEMENT AND PHARMACEUTICAL SALES

In pharmaceutical sales today there is much emphasis being placed on 'account planning, and account management'. This concept was previously applied to hospitals and PCTs since such organisations really were regarded as actual accounts. However, in an environment where access to primary care customers is now clearly diminishing (for sales professionals – not patients!), and where the market is becoming increasingly competitive, it has become quite relevant to regard GP practices as 'mini-accounts' in their own right. In this way, sales professionals can formulate account plans for each of their target customers.

An account plan can be regarded as a business plan for each key practice. The ultimate aim therefore, should be to outline action points for how you will leverage the various sources of prescribing influence which are discussed in the following chapters. In this context, success will invariably entail the following;

(i) Gaining access to the key prescribers
(ii) Positively influencing their prescribing habits

When all is said and done, this is exactly what your job is about. All the training, coaching and resources that are offered to you within your job, are provided to support you in ultimately meeting these two objectives.

Keeping the concept of account management in mind therefore, I have devised a simple model which I have called the *'GP circle of influence'* which I shall now discuss in further detail.

15. THE GP CIRCLE OF INFLUENCE

I now aim to cover key GP influences in further detail in order to help readers understand their importance, their respective roles and how exactly representatives can harness their potential. This is represented diagrammatically in figure 2 (below).

For clarity, this model will focus only on;

- Those variables upon which representative intervention will have the greatest impact
- Those variables which *all* primary care sales representatives will directly or indirectly be accountable for. (For example, I will not discuss dispensing practices because they are only found in certain parts of the country, and their existence requires a very different way of working to that of conventional 'ethical' pharmaceutical sales).

It is also important to note that figure 2 has been deliberately simplified since each factor represented will undoubtedly have its own list of influences. In this way, an 'influence-map' could theoretically be drawn for each variable in it's own right.

For absolute accuracy in relation to figure 2, it should be noted that in addition to influencing GPs, each factor *can*, and often does influence *other* factors within the model. Once again however, the rationale for this chapter is to focus solely on the influence which these factors have on GPs, which is why this particular dynamic will not be discussed here.

Finally, one may argue that the components of the third set of influences ('*other external influences*') cannot be affected by representatives. It is therefore fair to question why they have been included at all. However, it is not just the content of these factors which is important. It is the *emphasis* with which they are utilised that can determine how significantly they will influence customers. This level of emphasis is what *can* be affected by representatives (and certainly should be). Hence it is still as relevant to outline the nature of these factors as it is for the other entities covered in the chapter.

Figure 2 The GP circle of influence;

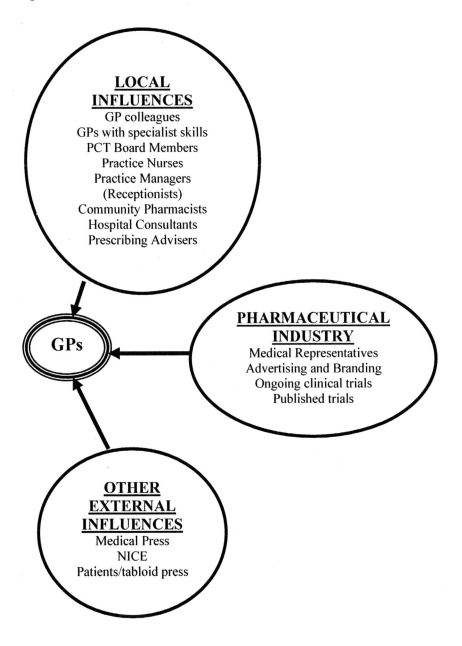

LOCAL
INFLUENCES
GP colleagues
GPs with specialist skills
PCT Board Members
Practice Nurses
Practice Managers
(Receptionists)
Community Pharmacists
Hospital Consultants
Prescribing Advisers

GPs

PHARMACEUTICAL
INDUSTRY
Medical Representatives
Advertising and Branding
Ongoing clinical trials
Published trials

OTHER
EXTERNAL
INFLUENCES
Medical Press
NICE
Patients/tabloid press

103

16. CLOSER LOOK AT THE INFLUENCERS

GENERAL PRACTITIONERS – (GPs)

At the hub of this model are of course the GPs themselves. For the primary care medical representative, these customers traditionally have been, and probably will for a long time, be the main individuals whom you will need to influence to increase the sales of your promoted products. The GPs are the focal members of all the stakeholders mentioned in this section, as it is they who will act upon these influences and translate them into prescribing choices at practice level.

GP COLLEAGUES

There are *many* reasons why GPs' prescribing habits may 'rub-off' on each other, so it is important to appreciate that GPs themselves are potential influencers as much as any other within this chapter.

This may be because GPs have trained together in the past, they may have qualified from the same medical institutions or they may attend meetings together. Alternatively, they may currently be working together (for example in the same practice, locality, or PCT). Whatever their 'common ground' is, it could ultimately provide for a significant level of peer influence.

The nature of this influence may range from simple professional respect for a colleague (e.g. *"Dr X is an esteemed colleague, so I follow what he prescribes"*), right up to unofficial 'peer-pressure' (e.g. *"Dr X prescribes this drug, so I feel obliged to follow his lead"*).

Also, in the case of practice partners there is of course the simple idea that if a GP wanted an *immediate* second opinion on a patient, then the easiest and quickest way to obtain one would probably be to ask a colleague in the same building!

Whatever the basis for this peer influence may be, it is important to acknowledge its existence, and try to tap into it wherever possible.

GPs WITH SPECIALIST SKILLS

In recent years, many GPs have taken on extra responsibilities in supporting hospital units to run clinics for out-patients. This is particularly common where GPs have obtained extra qualifications in specific medical fields, or have a specific interest in a particular clinical area. These GPs will usually be recognised by one of the following titles:

1. *Clinical Assistants* – these are GPs who spend an agreed number of days in a local hospital alongside a lead consultant for the relevant therapy area. The idea of them being based at the hospital clinic is that the consultant would always be on hand if the GP needed an immediate second opinion for a particular patient.
2. *GPs with Special Interests (also known as 'GPSis')*. These GPs will run supplementary clinics, although they may be based at their *own* practices *or* at the local hospitals depending on local arrangements. Neighbouring GPs will then refer patients to these GPSis who will either treat the patient themselves, or may then choose to refer the patient on to a hospital physician for a 'third' opinion (known as a tertiary referral).

These supplementary roles are proving to be invaluable to PCTs, because these GPs' expertise can be used to directly ease capacity issues for hospital clinics which otherwise have particularly long waiting lists.

Again – like consultants themselves, clinical assistants and GPSis are regarded as experts in their fields, so local GPs may well seek out *their* specialist opinions of particular drugs before making long term prescribing choices of their own.

Apart from obviously using your skills to ensure these specialists are users of your products, it would also be most advisable to use your knowledge of *their* positive opinions when speaking with *other* local GPs – particularly if these specialists endorse the use of your products. Once again, the best way to highlight their support of your products would be in formats such as speaker/clinical meetings where they can freely discuss their prescribing choices with groups of local prescribers. Otherwise, it may be beneficial just to mention (verbally) the patient populations where these GPSis and clinical assistants have found your drugs useful.

PCT BOARD MEMBERS

GPs will often take on extra responsibilities within their PCT to support them in achieving various clinical and organisational objectives for local medical care. In recent years, supplementary PCT roles will most often have taken the form of Professional Executive Committee (or 'PEC') membership.

One of the most important type of PEC members to pharmaceutical companies are *prescribing committee members.* These GPs are specifically responsible for meeting with fellow committee members on a periodic basis in order to evaluate the relative merits and drawbacks of individual drugs before deciding which ones to recommend on local prescribing guidelines. Other common board roles, or PEC Committee roles, may include those for clinical governance, medical education, commissioning and lead clinicians for particular diseases – such as cancer, coronary heart disease (CHD), diabetes and mental health.

The significance of these roles to medical representatives is that much like hospital consultants which are discussed later in this chapter, those GPs who sit on such PCT or PEC boards *may* be looked upon and respected by their peer GPs as being more specialised in particular areas. Their opinions may therefore have more credibility.

A possible way of using such professionals (both to develop them *and* to impart their knowledge and influence to your local customers) is to ask them to speak at lectures for local GPs (much like using speaker meetings led by consultants). Another method could be to ask them to 'chair' your speaker meetings on behalf of the consultant. Chairing speaker meetings usually comprises introducing the guest speaker, and facilitating a discussion amongst the group by fielding questions and answers between the speaker and audience members.

Using key GPs as chairmen will ensure that whilst you are using a local hospital opinion leader to endorse your product, you are also working alongside a respected local GP who himself may influence certain GPs if he is seen to be supportive of your company and your products.

PRACTICE NURSES

In an NHS system that is now being heavily strained by new primary care targets (as set out in the New GMS Contract), practice nurses are playing increasingly important roles in the provision of primary healthcare – this is undoubtedly the case in general chronic disease management, but is increasingly the case in prescribing too. In terms of chronic disease management, particular emphasis is being placed on conditions such as heart disease, asthma and diabetes. Within these expanded roles, practice nurses are typically taking on the following tasks;

- Routine monitoring of illnesses (e.g. monitoring blood sugar and blood pressure in diabetes)
- Routine monitoring of the effects of any prescribed drugs
- Looking after the patients general well being.

Because of this, many experienced practice nurses have now developed a robust knowledge of particular medical conditions, and of the drugs which are used to treat them.

During my time in primary care I regularly met practice nurses who were suggesting to GPs which medications should be prescribed to patients (despite them not having the direct authority to actually prescribe these drugs themselves). But because these GPs are fully aware of the extent to which nurses have developed their knowledge in this way, many of them are willing to trust their clinical choices (albeit the final prescribing decision still resides with the GP).

How this can manifest itself (and what I have heard happen on numerous occasions) is that a nurse will see a patient, diagnose the condition, and will then actually write out a prescription for a chosen drug – including full dosing information. The nurse will then take the prescription to the doctor and will very briefly explain to the doctor what he/she has decided for the patient based on the diagnosis – if the GP agrees with the nurses chosen course of action, he will simply sign the prescription. Interestingly, and more often than not – GPs will regularly verify the clinical judgement of their practice nurses in this way.

In addition to responsibilities taken on through chronic disease management, practice nurses are now also taking on more of a role in dealing with minor ailments. This is often done through 'triage' type systems, whereby a patient's first contact within a surgery will be with a nurse who will try and diagnose and often deal with an acute problem in order to ease capacity issues on GP time. Again, this would mean that such nurses could be in a very favourable position to influence medication choice.

In this way it is clear to see that depending on which therapy area you are promoting in, the level of contact that nurses now have with patients, coupled with the working relationships which many nurses have with their GP colleagues, means that the scope for them to influence prescribing is rapidly expanding. This makes them a very important customer group to focus on when looking at the circle of influence.

In my experience however, it is worth bearing in mind that the exact level of influence in this type of relationship will vary from one practice to the next. Some GPs are more than happy (and even sometimes relieved!) to be able to hand prescribing responsibilities over to their nurses, whereas GPs in other practices will not want to give over such autonomy. It is therefore well worthwhile to try and establish (in *each* of your key practices) what the exact relationship is between individual nurses and GPs. This will enable you to benefit from the potential rewards from working with *both* of these key customers where relevant.

PRACTICE MANAGERS

Practice managers really are the hub of the practice in terms of how it functions day to day. Many people would assume that since GPs are the ones who administer medical care that they are at the centre of everything, but in reality I have worked with practice managers who appear to know *almost everything* about the functioning of each 'sub-team' within the practice, whereas doctors, nurses and receptionists tend to be most aware only of *their own* immediate functional priorities and issues. This means that practice managers can be very useful allies to have in a practice – especially those where you will need to understand their issues better in order to work more effectively with the key prescribers.

It is amazing how many valuable nuggets of information can be uncovered in this manner. The skill of the medical salesperson therefore, is to use these scatterings of information to 'piece together' a more complete picture of how a practice is functioning; what are its strengths, weaknesses, issues and needs?

If you can leverage and use this information in the right way, it really will help you to engage your prescribers far more effectively when you *do* eventually get to see them. Therefore as opposed to being seen as *'any other sales rep'* you will then be viewed as someone more professional who has taken time and effort to learn about what exact circumstances and work challenges the practice is facing. This all counts towards gaining credibility and building more robust relationships with key prescribers. Also, knowing more about a practice in such ways can aid you in making better business decisions when developing practice account plans.

Another way in which medical representatives can work with practice managers is to utilise them to initiate key projects within the practice. They may well be the ideal person to introduce value-added services to the practice (such as auditing, and training sessions). You will often find that if you are trying to introduce such offerings to a practice, then the practice manager can be a great internal ally since they could champion the idea to GPs. This is particularly useful in a situation where the partners would otherwise refuse the offering because they are not willing to see you in the first instance.

I have tended to find over the years, that practice managers are often willing to interact with industry professionals more so than surgery receptionists are, and in some cases more so than the doctors themselves.

In some rare circumstances, you may even find that some practice managers are quite active in direct prescribing influence over their GPs. It may be for example, that they have taken a strong interest in monitoring the prescribing of their GPs after a pharmaceutical adviser visit, or after analysing some Prescribing Analysis and CosT (PACT) data. Once again therefore – much like the receptionist, the practice manager is someone who should be regarded as a key professional with whom working relationships must be cultivated.

THE SURGERY RECEPTIONIST

I can sense some readers raising their eyebrows at the notion of how a receptionist can influence prescribing – DON'T! The surgery receptionist is affectionately nicknamed *'the dragon at the gate'* by many representatives! Remember – as I have said previously, your two objectives in this job are to *access* your customers, and to use this access to *positively influence your customers' prescribing habits*. The trouble in addressing the latter objective, is that all too often, the *receptionist* is the one who stands between you and your ability to influence that doctor (and boy, do some of them like to stand between you and the doctor!)

I was once asked to take part in a pilot project to develop ideas which will aid access with key GPs. We explored various initiatives which may help us in accessing key customers, yet a consistently resounding theme that came out of this project was the age-old need to nurture and cultivate relationships with receptionists since they are widely recognised as having such a major influence on access to customers.

An interesting piece of research conducted by Doctors.net.uk[5] sampled 500 GP respondents to find out *why* they see medical representatives. Of these 500 GPs, 250 actually said that they were happy to let their *receptionist* 'choose' which representatives got to see them – whether this be through appointment or spec calls. So as much as salespeople like to think that it is long standing relationships with GPs which enable us to access them, this research is actually testament to how much influence *receptionists* can have on GP access.

So if you can get *these* particular stakeholders on your side then you are winning half the battle, since very basically and very obviously, how can you be expected to influence the prescribing choice of a doctor if you cannot even get to see him? It is clear that influencing prescribing within a practice is becoming a more complex process, and you may therefore find that you need to see more than just one GP to exert full prescribing influence over an entire practice.

Therefore because receptionists represent the primary liaison point of the *whole* practice, I believe it makes much better sense to regard front desk staff as being

---

[5] *'Why do GPs see representatives?'* November 2004: doctors.net.uk

members of the practice team just like any other professional, and it is therefore important to build up a rapport with *them* as much as it is important to do so with your prescribers!

COMMUNITY PHARMACISTS

At present, the community pharmacist (like many other stakeholders in this chapter), can randomly be found to have *any* level of influence on GP prescribing. Traditionally, I have also observed that pharmacists have felt fairly neglected by the drug industry in general. This is probably due to the very fact that their exact role on prescribing influence has not been clearly established till now. In essence I have found that many pharmacists have similar motivations to GPs for seeing medical representatives – they are mainly interested in being kept updated with new drug developments.

Those companies who have over-the-counter (OTC) reps *will* make regular contact with pharmacists for consumer products such as toothpastes, soaps, cosmetics etc. Medical representatives who promote prescription medicines however (often referred to by pharmacists as 'ethical' reps) have traditionally visited pharmacists for two broad business needs: to obtain information relating to local prescribing patterns, and to drive general awareness of therapeutic choices within drug classes.

In terms of the first point, pharmacists have always been a valuable source of information for medical representatives. This information can relate directly to GP prescribing, since you will find that all pharmacists will practice in close proximity to a GP surgery, and will therefore tend to manage a significant throughput of patients from these local practices. Because of this, pharmacists tend to build up a fairly accurate picture of

GP prescribing habits. If you can therefore develop good enough relationships with these pharmacists, then they may be willing to give you clues as to what, and how these GPs are prescribing within particular therapy areas. As I explained in chapter 3, we as industry professionals, will never be privy to exact/ individual GP prescribing patterns, so in the absence of speaking to GPs themselves, pharmacist's knowledge can be a vital source of information in attempting to understand our target customers' prescribing habits.

Whether or not a pharmacist chooses to share this information with you however, is purely down to their discretion. During my career I have inevitably been 'shouted-out' of one or two shops by pharmacists who have been angered and offended by the fact that I have attempted to request such information from them! My advice would be to use tact when deciding *which* pharmacists to extrapolate this information from, since not all of them are open to sharing this knowledge with medical representatives.

As part of the ABPI rules, medical representatives are not allowed to have any contact with patients for the purpose of product promotion. This is because adverts to patients could result in them requesting medications which are clinically inappropriate for them, despite the fact that they may perceive there to be some benefit in them receiving it. This would clearly create undue pressure both on the workload of doctors, and on a doctor's clinical judgement (patient influence is discussed in more depth towards the end of this chapter). Therefore, the second way in which community pharmacists have traditionally been involved in pharmaceutical prescribing, is through driving awareness of therapeutic choices to both patients and doctors.

For example, pharmacists may informally assess selected patient groups to determine which ones could benefit from a change of treatment. The pharmacist then uses his professional judgement to inform these patients that an alternative medication is available. Additionally, some pharmacists have good enough communication channels established with local GPs for them to simply telephone the doctor to recommend that a medication change be effected there and then.

Many GPs would actually welcome such input from pharmacists because such suggestions may result in patients benefiting from a 'streamlining' of medications – this could be a 'win' for the patient (as they may then be changed to a simpler dosing schedule for example), and it would be a 'win' for the GP – since the streamlining may result in lower drug costs.

Another way in which pharmacists are in a unique position to influence prescribing is via the 'repeat prescribing' process. Vast numbers of patients in the NHS today receive repeat medications. This situation arises where patients are started on a long term course of medication for a particular condition. Once the drug has been shown to have a satisfactory effect, the patient no longer needs to see the GP regularly and is therefore automatically issued with a repeat prescription e.g. every month.

However, what occasionally happens is that the drug causes the patient to develop side effects which they may not associate with the drug. They will therefore carry on taking it and suffering the side effect. Also, because the patient does *not* now have to see the doctor in order to receive the medication, they are unable to raise this issue with him.

This is where the community pharmacist can intervene. Whilst the patient will no longer liaise with the *doctor,* they WILL nonetheless be seeing the *pharmacist* regularly in order to have the drug dispensed. Therefore the patient may either mention the occurrence of the side effect in passing to the pharmacist, or the pharmacist may proactively probe the patient to uncover the potential occurrence of such side effects.

Either way, if a pharmacist is bought-into the benefits of *your* drug, they could well suggest to the doctor and/or the patient that their current medication should be replaced with *your* brand of drug. Hence this is *another* situation where the pharmacist may take the proactive step of speaking to the GP about arranging for the patient's medication to be changed over immediately.

Despite these potential benefits however, some medical representatives still believe that the above methods of driving business are actually too slow, too indirect and generally less dynamic than influencing prescribers directly. This may be true, but until now it is fair to say that there has been no particular incentive or contractual requirement for pharmacists to make such interventions.

The introduction of the New Community Pharmacy Contract[8] however, may well signal a change in this dynamic. The reason for this is that much like the recent GMS contract for GPs (discussed in chapter 9), the new pharmacy contract has been designed to give greater ownership to community pharmacists in the improvement of public health.

As part of this new contract, community pharmacists' payments will now be directed towards the quality of care and services which they provide, as opposed to payments being driven by the volume of prescriptions which they dispense[6]. Under this contract, community pharmacists will potentially be able to offer a number of extra services[7] such as;

- Medication reviews which (as highlighted earlier) have been formulated to aid GPs in detecting various drug therapy issues such as the occurrence of unwanted side effects
- Screening for undiagnosed conditions
- Supplementary/Repeat Prescribing
- Smoking Cessation Advice
- Lifestyle modification advice (such as dietary and exercise guidance)
- Advice on over the counter medicines which are suitable for self-limiting conditions, as well as advice on other remedies to aid recovery from minor illnesses
- Contraception services
- Anti-coagulant (anti blood clotting) monitoring
- Clinics for conditions such as diabetes

From the government and NHS viewpoint, the New Community Pharmacy Contract has been designed to meet a number of healthcare needs:

1. Pharmacists are highly qualified and educated professionals whose knowledge and expertise is perceived to have been sub-utilised for years, since they are currently only acting as drug dispensers – a job which requires little technical expertise. The new pharmacy contract *will* however encourage pharmacists (and their staff) to use their clinical knowledge and diagnostic

---

[6] *'Framework For A New Community Pharmacy Contract'* July 2003, RCGP Summary Paper 2003/13: www.rcgp.org.uk
[7] *'Dawn of a new era for pharmacy'* 1st April 2005, Department Of Health: www.dh.gov.uk

skills much more so than before. It is felt that utilising pharmacist skills in this way will not only boost morale of the profession in general, but will also serve to provide the public with a greater pool of medical professionals from which high quality healthcare can be accessed.

2. Patients are now at increased risk from potentially fatal undiagnosed conditions such as high cholesterol, high blood pressure and diabetes (mainly because these conditions are largely 'asymptomatic'). Therefore those pharmacists who can diagnose these conditions *themselves* may well be able to offer medical intervention to those patients who have previously 'slipped through the GPs' net'. In this way pharmacists can play a major role in the improvement of public health.

3. Those patients who *have* been diagnosed, and are now established on treatments may be at increased risk of suffering drug side effects, and drug-to-drug interactions if they are taking many medicines for different conditions (as discussed above). Therefore pharmacists are in a very prominent position to be able to detect such medication errors.

4. The NHS are trying to cut down on the prescribing of medications which are not clinically essential for patients. Such prescribing may occur (for example) in situations where patients have previously been started on a drug for an 'acute' (or short term) problem, but are now being issued with repeat prescriptions where it is not necessarily required. This is a concept known as 'medicines management' and is a key focus of the new contract for general practitioners too. It is therefore seen that pharmacists can offer support to these streamlining processes.

5. Overall, GP workloads can be tangibly reduced if pharmacists can take on some of the extra responsibilities highlighted above.

In the above ways, and *particularly* through the new pharmacy contract, it is clear to see how pharmacist intervention on drug prescribing is actually becoming more formalised. It is also interesting to note the specific therapy areas which this will most likely impact upon – most notably diabetes, heart disease, asthma and contraception.

With the changing role of the community pharmacist therefore, those representatives who work towards building long term relations with pharmacists from now, will clearly be in a more favourable position once pharmacists *do* become more integrated into the delivery of public health in primary care through the full implementation of *their* new contract.

HOSPITAL PHYSICIANS

The choice of drugs which local hospital doctors make can hugely impact on your own customers' prescribing choice. It is for this reason that hospital consultants are such important stakeholders in the circle of influence.

At this point, it is relevant for me to briefly clarify two key hospital roles to readers – that of consultants, *and* professors. Simply put, a professor can be described as a consultant who has attained further qualifications, to a point where they are at the pinnacle of their knowledge within a therapy area. A professor is usually based at a hospital, and will work in the capacity of a consultant too. Therefore whilst it is very important to recognise the difference in qualifications (and therefore seniority) between consultants and professors, it is nonetheless fair to cluster these professionals together for the sake of this particular book.

By virtue of the fact that these prescribers are called *consultants*, they are clearly experts in their chosen fields, and far from having the stresses of practicing *general* medicine like your average GP, consultants will have spent years developing specialised knowledge and skills within one particular therapy area. It has been said that GPs are having to learn *'less and less about more and more'*, whilst consultants have perfected the art of learning *'more and more about less and less!'* It is for this reason that when GPs want to seek a more in depth opinion on a particular therapy area, the respective consultants are often in the strongest position to give this advice.

As stated previously, you may have some responsibility for directly influencing hospital doctors as part of your 'afternoon' activity – this will depend on the structure of your salesforce;

- Some companies will leave the responsibility for hospitals solely with the primary care representatives
- Some will use a combination of primary care *and* hospital representatives
- Other companies will choose to leave *all* hospital promotional activity to a dedicated hospital representative.

Therefore even if you are given no direct responsibility to liaise with hospital doctors/consultants, then you certainly will be responsible for how you use these physicians' views of your drug when conversing with your GPs. In this way, it is recognised that the way in which you either maximise a consultant's *positive* endorsement, or minimise a consultant's *lack of* endorsement is a direct responsibility of the primary care medical representative.

Your skill as the salesperson therefore, will be to identify *which* local consultants are actively prescribing and endorsing the use of your drug, and then to ensure that your GPs are fully aware of this. In this way, the consultant's opinions can be used with your customers as a credible form of endorsement. This type of support can be very powerful since it is local to the GP, *yet* it is independent in its allegiance (as it is not coming from someone who works for your company).

It is important to recognise however, that some GPs may value the opinions of *certain* consultants more so than others. The reasons for this preference may originate from any of the following;

- A GP may have worked under a particular consultant during their own medical training, so they will feel more strongly affiliated with them
- The GP may have had a good experience of a consultant through a past patient referral which was dealt with particularly well
- A GP may have attended a lecture given by a consultant which they found to be particularly convincing
- A GP may simply trust the opinion of *another* GP who respects a particular consultant
- A GP may have read articles which have been written by a particular consultant
- Some consultants often take on a number of extra roles over and above their basic job which gives them further credibility (such as roles with PCTs, NICE or other clinical bodies). This again, can add to their credibility as opinion leaders

- Some consultants (depending on the therapy area) may run clinics directly in primary care settings – a concept known as 'outreach clinics'. The purpose of these clinics may be to ease referral times for hospital outpatients or simply for consultants to work with practices who have requested direct support in setting up patient care initiatives. Either way, this is another way in which a GP may become more familiar and affiliated with a particular consultant.

Above, I have suggested that it is essential for new representatives to highlight *which* local consultants are endorsing the use of your products. I would also suggest however, that it is essential to do another piece of background work – that is to find out *which of the local consultants tend to influence your target* GPs – *regardless* of what these consultants' opinions of your product are. This is useful as it can help you (and/or your hospital representative) to think about *which* consultants it would be most beneficial to start developing.

When I was selling a cardiovascular drug to hospital consultants I can recall moving to a new hospital territory in which I had to carry out such a task. I was surprised to find out that in this new area, it was actually an Elderly Care (geriatric) Consultant who was the most eminent and respected hospital physician – even though one would expect the Cardiologist (heart specialist) to be the most influential consultant in the context of selling a cardiovascular drug.

In those cases where consultant opinions are *particularly* favourable towards your drug, it can be of benefit to arrange for consultants to make contact with local GPs so that the primary care prescribers can be made aware of the consultant's opinion of your drug. This can be done in a number of ways, though these will generally be based around the format of a *speaker meeting.*

The concept of speaker meetings is simply where an audience of GPs, will be invited to a lecture or discussion which is given by a consultant. Such meetings are generally one to two hours in length, and are based around a discussion of a particular disease or therapy area. These meetings therefore tend to have an educational content, though it is acceptable for the consultant to also discuss your drug in context of where it fits into the treatment of the condition in question. Organising such an event can have a two-fold benefit;

1. If GPs are exposed to consultants who strongly endorse the use of your product, then these GPs are more likely to follow their prescribing choices
2. Secondly, using your consultants in this way will help to develop the links which *your company* has *with the consultant.* This helps to build stronger working relationships with the consultant over the longer term.

Using the opinions of consultants in this way can be a powerful tool for influencing large numbers of prescribers, but it is important to bear in mind that consultants tend to be extremely conscious about the integrity of their clinical views. So whilst using them *can* be influential, it should also be recognised that the backlash from misrepresenting their views can be just as impactful. What I mean by this is that consultant habits must always be accurately represented to prescribers if you are using their opinions as a 'third party recommendation'.

PRESCRIBING ADVISERS

Prescribing advisers (sometimes known as pharmaceutical advisers, or Pas) play a vital role in advising GPs on which drugs to prescribe in particular therapy areas. They are employed directly by PCTs since a large part of PCT policy relates to the control of GP prescribing in order to reduce excess expenditure of this resource. There are two things that make the role of the PA unique;

1. They are the *only* stakeholder in this model who are *directly* responsible for influencing GP prescribing.
2. Secondly, they do not have direct contact with patients (unlike most of the other individual stakeholders in this model). This is because the vast majority of their work is carried out in an advisory and management capacity.

In order for pharmaceutical advisers to supervise GP prescribing, some of their responsibilities include;

- Developing drug formularies (as discussed in chapter 10) which may be done in conjunction with local hospitals
- Monitoring levels of generic prescribing (as discussed in chapter 7)
- Reducing prescribing of particular drug groups (such as anti-biotics)
- Generally working towards lowering drug expenditure within their PCTs.

It is extremely rare that a primary care representative will have *any* direct contact with a PA since liaising with this level of professional requires a drastically different approach to that which primary care representatives are trained in. For example, it would be highly inappropriate to 'detail' a prescribing adviser in the way that you may do for other stakeholders. This is why it is usually the job of your HDM to call on these professionals.

If drugs *are* to be discussed with prescribing advisers, their areas of interest in a drug would tend to be in a combination of *evidence based* and *economic* terms. In the context of prescribing advisers however, the concept of drug economics goes far beyond just talking about the monthly cost of a drug (as you would do with GPs), but might actually mean discussing geographical cost models for complete primary care trusts, in order to establish what financial impact a drug may have if it were to be prescribed across an *entire* district.

For example, IF it could be demonstrated that using your drug may prove to reduce costs in *other* areas of expenditure within a PCT (such as by reducing the rate of hospital referrals or actual hospitalisations), then the prescribing adviser may actually take steps to formally advise GPs that *your* drug *should* proactively be prescribed. If such guidance *is* ever given, then it is possible that other drugs in the same class will not be endorsed by the PA in an effort to streamline overall prescribing within their district. This will usually be communicated through a formulary, guideline, protocol or other type of prescribing guidance (as suggested in chapter 10).

Once again, it is worth mentioning that if your drug *isn't* endorsed by a PA, this can have a very damaging effect on your territory sales potential. Consequently, if your drug *were* to be endorsed in this manner, then it could hugely accelerate your sales. To add a little reality to this scenario however, it should once again be remembered that different PCTs have different levels of uptake and compliance to prescribing guidance. Therefore if your drug *isn't* endorsed it is not necessarily the end of the road for you!

MEDICAL REPRESENTATIVES

Under this heading, it is important to appreciate that when describing the influence of medical representatives, this will mean influence by yourself *and* of course your competitors. The way in which representatives will influence GP prescribing will be through face to face calls in GP practices, or by a variety of meeting formats including the following;

- *Surgery meetings.* This is where you may be asked to provide lunch for the doctors in respect of the time you take up to sell your products. This will usually consist of a simple sandwich/cold snack lunch.
- *Evening meetings.* As discussed in chapter 2, much is said and written about the ethics of evening meetings. Many believe that these are used as vehicles by which representatives will 'wine and dine' doctors as a form of corporate hospitality. In this way, some argue that this itself is a way of unethically enticing prescribing. In reality however, the evening meeting concept came about simply as an extension of the lunch-meeting concept – the difference being that due to time constraints, doctors may not be able to accommodate your visits during mornings *or* lunches, and are therefore given the option to discuss your products during a dinner slot where they may be able to spare *more* time. Once again, it is worth emphasising that the ABPI code of practice states that "...any subsistence must be strictly limited to the main purpose of the event and be secondary to the purpose of the meeting."[1] It is my belief that if you

really want to have more in-depth clinical discussions with customers in order to build stronger professional relationships with them, then evening meetings are the most effective way to do this. This is simply because doctors tend to be much more focussed on *your* interaction when taken away from the stresses of the surgery environment itself.

- *Speaker meetings.* These are generally used to facilitate an interaction between your GP customers and a local consultant/opinion leader. This can be a very powerful way of driving your sales. Speaker meetings are discussed in more depth under the heading of 'Hospital Physicians' below.

- *Exhibition meetings.* This is where you would arrange a display stand with your promotional literature. You would then pay an agreed fee to an event organiser in lieu of the exhibition space. Your presence at such events would normally be secondary to a pre-organised medical/clinical meeting, therefore your time with customers tends to be over a coffee or a lunch break. It is for this reason that these meetings can be an awkward type of environment in which to try and engage customers into effective selling discussions. I therefore believe that these meetings are best used for just three basic requirements. *Firstly,* they may be used to meet customers who may not otherwise see representatives in their practices, because many of them are actually happy to accommodate discussions with representatives at such events since they are not under the same time pressure as when they are in their clinics. *Secondly,* they are a good way of maximising promotion of a new product or indication at a time when all that is required to increase sales are quick reminders – a concept often referred to as *'making noise'* in the market place. The final benefit of exhibition meetings is the opportunity of gaining 'call-backs' – a technique where you use your time with the doctors to gain commitment for them to see you back in their practices at a later date.

Companies recognise that using a combination of 'face to face' *and* meeting contacts represents an effective promotional mix to be able to sell to most customers. Because of this, companies will set aside a meetings budget which will be allocated to you on an annual basis. You will then be given a degree of autonomy in how you intend to use your budget in order to effectively maximise promotion.

Looking back at figure 2 you will see that as a medical representative, whilst your means of influencing a GP will only be through the contact types mentioned herein, you will also be responsible for how you develop and use as many of the other influences described *below* as possible. Remember, this is a multi-faceted job, and due to the inability of being able to pinpoint *exactly* what influences a GPs prescribing decision, it is your job to work on as many of these variables as possible in order to maximise your territory sales.

ADVERTISING AND BRANDING

Pharmaceutical advertising and branding can have a huge impact on prescribing, and in the absence of medical sales professionals, this is arguably the only medium by which pharmaceutical companies can *directly* reach and influence prescribers.

Although the actual development of advertising campaigns are beyond the remit of medical representatives, I strongly believe that we nonetheless have a direct responsibility in ensuring that prescribers are exposed to product advertising and branding through the promotional literature which is provided to us. I can remember right back to my own first training course where the following concept was continually drilled into our heads;

- If a GP HEARS you selling a clinical message, they will remember *some* of it
- If a GP SEES the product's advertising images, they will retain *more* of the message
- If however, the GP sees **AND** hears the product being sold to them, these marketing messages will have the greatest memorability.

It is for this reason that I firmly believe that promotional material and literature must be used in EVERY sales call. Medical representatives are the only people who have the opportunity of ensuring that prescribers see AND hear sales messages synergistically.

I would even suggest that if you are not intending to deliver a full-on 'cover-to-cover' product detail to a customer, it is still important to at least keep a sales aid within their line of vision during the discussion, so that the brand visuals are recorded into the customer's subconscious memory. This also applies to exhibition-type meetings where branded display panels should *always* be on show, in order to imprint brand images into the minds of your customers. This all helps towards overall brand familiarity, brand recall and ultimately, prescribing choice.

With regards to the rest of the advertising mix (such as that which will be carried in the medical press), this will be developed and implemented by your marketing department and will only serve to complement the work which *you* will be doing when in front of your customers.

CLINICAL PAPERS AND THE MEDICAL PRESS

Clinical papers are a fundamental element of pharmaceuticals, and they probably represent the most important tool of a salespersons trade in pharmaceutical sales! Clinical trials will form the bedrock of *any* marketing campaign since promotional claims can only be made if they are verified by scientific evidence.

Because they are so important, you will undoubtedly be given specific guidance on how your company wants you to use the clinical studies which are available for your promoted products. Therefore the scope of this section is simply to explain the key principles of clinical papers in general terms.

As already outlined, clinical papers will form the clinical evidence base for your promoted products. They are the 'black and white' proof that a product has gone through the necessary clinical tests in real patients in order to primarily demonstrate three key things;

1. They can improve a medical condition which the molecule has specifically been developed for
2. They do this safely, without causing life threatening side effects
3. The final requirement is to prove that neither of the *above* are 'chance' findings – i.e. both findings must be 'statistically significant' enough to rule out the possibility of coincidences which appear to favour the drug.

In simple terms you can regard clinical papers as being the verified proof that your product actually performs to a standard that is claimed by the drug manufacturers. It is metaphorically similar to adverts on the television for consumer goods such as toothpastes, shampoos and other products. When any claims are made relating to the performance of such consumer goods, they will have to have been substantiated by unambiguous product tests which prove these outcomes.

In much the same way, clinical papers are the equivalent vehicles used in pharmaceuticals.

The studies which demonstrate the three requirements mentioned above are then used either to apply for clinical licenses, or are used as part of a clinical evidence portfolio upon which a drug will be competitively promoted to clinicians and to prescribing authorities. (In the UK, licenses are applied for via the Medicines and Healthcare products Regulatory Agency, or 'MHRA').

After these basic requirements have been proven, further trials will be conducted in order to determine extra clinical benefits relating to the disease or condition. Also, depending on the relevance of the therapy area, further trials may be carried out to prove long term benefits ranging from quality of life improvements, right up to the improvement of actual survival (known as a mortality study). The results of these subsequent studies may then be used to support applications for further clinical licenses for the product.

In order to maintain credibility in pharmaceutical sales, the ABPI stipulate that ANY claim which is made about an aspect of a drug's performance *must* be fully substantiated by a clinical study. In addition, it should be noted that those studies which highlight a drug's benefits in unlicensed indications can only be presented to clinicians on request – i.e. they cannot be proactively presented during sales discussions as this could mislead clinicians into believing that a drug *is* licensed in particular conditions where it actually is *not*.

An interesting point to note is that some of the clinical *journals* in which these trials are actually published, are particulariy well respected in their own right. Such is the reputation of some of these journals therefore, that just to have a trial reviewed in one of them could be of competitive advantage within itself. This is for two reasons – firstly (as stated) there is undoubtedly a 'halo effect' which is associated with being mentioned in highly reputed journals, but secondly an obvious competitive advantage comes from the sheer volume of readership which is achieved by these journals. In this country, the Lancet and the New England Journal of Medicine (NEJM) are amongst the most esteemed medical journals in circulation.

One of my senior hospital customers once said that if he wanted to keep up to date on *non*-clinical issues such as the NHS structure and 'medical politics', then he would read one particular set of journals, but if he wanted high quality, authentic scientific commentaries of the latest medical trial work, then he would only look to the Lancet or the NEJM.

The importance of clinical papers in pharmaceutical sales means that their influence stretches far beyond primary care. The outcomes of clinical studies can actually determine guidance given by top advisory bodies such as NICE. In some cases, clinical studies can be so influential that they have been known to shape *entire* pharmaceutical markets – even on a global scale.

A classic example of this came in the mid 1990's when three major trials were published which demonstrated clear, improved outcomes for patients taking statins (a class of drugs used to lower cholesterol, which were new at the time). The trials in question were the '4S'[8], 'WOSCOPS'[9] and 'CARE'[10] studies. These studies quite

[8] 4S Group, The Lancet 1994; 344: 1383-89
[9] Shepherd et. al, New England Journal of Medicine 1995; 333: 1301-7
[10] Sacks et. al. New England Journal of Medicine 1996; 335: 1001-9

literally revolutionised the market for cholesterol lowering drugs, and the explosion of statin sales is largely attributable to these key trials. This has now become the single largest therapy area of all in the global pharmaceutical market. Yet ironically, before these studies were published there was still open debate as to whether or not these drugs actually offered *any* benefits at all to heart patients.

In summary therefore, the clinical evidence base of a drug can make or break its future sales potential – both in *what* the study results show, and in *how* well clinicians are made aware of the studies – because as with anything in business, if a product has been shown to be competitively superior, then this fact needs to be exposed to target audiences as widely, and as robustly as possible – there will be no point in keeping it a secret!

NICE

The National Institute for Health and Clinical Excellence, or NICE (previously known as the National Institute for Clinical Excellence) is an independent organisation which is responsible for providing national guidance both on the *promotion of good health* and on the *prevention and treatment of ill health*[11].

As part of their role, NICE evaluates the clinical and cost effectiveness of drugs, diagnostic tests and surgical (or interventional) procedures. The scope of their work is therefore reflected in the term 'health technology appraisal' which succinctly describes what they cover. The guidance issued by NICE applies to England and Wales. The equivalent clinical body in Scotland is the Scottish Intercollegiate Guidelines Network (SIGN).

---

[11] National Institute for Health and Clinical Excellence: www.nice.org.uk

NICE tends to review around 50 'technologies' (or drugs) per year, and the criteria for determining which ones are selected for appraisal, tend to be those which fall under the following categories;

- Those which address *major* public health problems
- Those which may cause problems in how they are managed upon their launch (e.g. if they are used in therapy areas which have previously had no independent guidelines issued)
- Or those which come at a significant cost to the NHS (e.g. cancer treatments)

In addition, NICE will most often review medicines when there is uncertainty surrounding the use of a particular drug or drug class. Such uncertainty may result in varied uptake of the drug across the country, and NICEs role in this scenario is to alleviate this uncertainty and ensure that those treatments which are adjudged to be safe and effective are recommended to patients across the *entire* country rather than in isolation. Because of the above, it is *newer* drugs which more often tend to be the subject of NICE appraisals. The idea therefore, is that NICE can direct prescribers as to the most suitable use of a drug at a time when physicians themselves will inevitably be trying to understand where best, such new treatments should fit in to clinical practice.

In evaluating *new* medicines in this way therefore, NICE will also assess the best practice use of *existing* medicines in the same class. This means that NICE will often develop clinical guidelines for *entire* therapy areas which encompass both new *and* existing therapies within a class.

Once again, the limitations of medical representatives' influence over NICE are similar to that which were described in the previous section on prescribing advisers, in that you as a medical representative are almost certain never to come into direct contact with a member of NICE since they are made up of a highly specialised panel of medics and advisers. (The only rare exception to this rule may be if such a panel member were to also work as a local physician for example).

So whilst you cannot influence the *actual guidance which is given* by NICE, you can of course fully control the way in which you *use* this guidance to influence your customers' prescribing choices.

Technically speaking, it is not mandatory for GPs to adhere to the guidance which is given by NICE, but since PCTs develop their own clinical guidelines and protocols to complement NICE, it is assumed that GPs should adhere to these recommendations. Therefore if *any* of your promoted products have been positively endorsed by NICE, it would be highly advisable to mention this fact in *every* call!

PATIENT INFLUENCE AND THE NATIONAL TABLOID PRESS

It should be noted that the ability of primary care representatives to affect patient influence on GPs is virtually zero! This is because (as discussed previously in this chapter), drug representative-to-patient contact is strictly forbidden under the ABPI code of practice. In relevance to this book however, it is still very important to acknowledge that patient influence *does exist*, as it is rapidly increasing.

There is a saying in business that *the customer is always right!* In the context of medicine, patients can be regarded as a doctor's customer. In this way therefore, doctors are of course working to serve patient needs, but the biggest difference in medicine is that patients are definitely NOT *always* right! This is simply because medicine is such a specialised area – therefore doctors need to take very careful steps before they give any medical advice, or prescribing any medicines to patients.

Despite this, many of my customers have long complained about the fact patients too often believe that *they* know what is best for them without actually knowing and understanding the clinical background of their symptoms and illnesses.

I have often heard of patient influence manifesting itself in the following ways;

- Some patients will use the internet to research their illnesses and then request their GPs to take particular courses of action – e.g. they may insist on a secondary referral to another doctor, or they may insist on receiving a particular drug which they have read about on the web.
- Other patients may spontaneously read about a *'new wonder drug'* which is documented in the national tabloid press, and immediately demand that they be prescribed this treatment too
- Some patients are known to be 'regular visitors' to a practice, so this in itself may pressure a GP into looking harder for a quick cure to satisfy them
- Some patients will often insist on receiving a particular medication which they have successfully used in the past themselves, and therefore believe they need to take again (e.g. anti-biotics)
- In some cases, patients may even request a drug if they have heard that a friend or relative is taking it – (quite frighteningly, I have even heard of patients who partake in pill-swapping to experiment if their friend's drugs will work on them!)

In any of the above scenarios the major challenge which medical professionals now face is the fact that these courses of action are very often *inappropriate* for these patients, despite them believing the contrary. The GP is then left in a difficult situation whereby he either has to 'give in' to the patient's requests, or have a potential conflict with the patient who may not appreciate why the GP has refused their requests.

I have previously come across GPs who deal with such pressures in *both* of the ways described above – i.e. those who *will* accept the patient's request, and those who *will not* change their clinical decisions despite such patient pressure. The former type of GPs feel that they are so busy in their overall work, that they simply do not have the time to argue with patients, so will just agree to the requests. The other extreme of GP tends to take great offence to the fact that a patient has taken it upon themselves to give the GP suggestions as to what courses of action to take, and will therefore resolutely stick to his own clinical judgement in the face of such pressure.

In either case it is useful to appreciate that with recent advances in the way which information is accessible to the public (namely through the internet), the influence of this stakeholder group is visibly growing, and whilst many medical practitioners resent this form of influence, many other GPs are actually embracing the interest which patients are taking in their own conditions, and have used this to encourage patients to take more ownership of their illnesses – especially in high risk areas such as heart disease and diabetes, where much of the necessary treatment requires changes in patient lifestyles – through dieting, exercising and smoking cessation – factors which can *only* be affected by patients themselves.

17. GENERAL THREATS TO YOUR BUSINESS

I now aim to examine just *some* of the many factors which pose a threat to your chances of success – you will see that some factors present a *direct* threat to your business, whilst others will create indirect threats.

COMPETITORS AND THEIR PRODUCTS

The availability of competitor products creates extra choice for GPs when prescribing, and this in itself is an obvious threat to your business.

Most pharmaceutical managers and marketers will argue that their product is the best on the market. Of course, there are *some* drug classes where products are genuinely, and undeniably distinct in terms of their efficacy and/or their safety. Furthermore, there may be other situations whereby delivery systems for drugs (e.g. new asthma inhaler devices) may make a product tangibly, and genuinely unique. However, there are still many *other* drug classes in existence which tend to be made up of very similar products, which therefore are *not* so clinically distinct. This often results in a number of products in one class being equally effective, equally safe and quite often, similarly priced.

The problem which this presents therefore, is that despite the best intentions and strongest arguments put forward by pharmaceutical sales and marketing, many customers will still *perceive* product offerings to be similar, and sometimes even indistinguishable. Doctors often use the term 'class effect' which represents their perception of such similarities. They will therefore use this term to justify why they change from one product to another without any great consideration, or 'brand loyalty'.

For instance, if a patient presented to a doctor with basic hypertension (high blood pressure), there are well in excess of 200 different drugs which the doctor could justifiably prescribe in order to treat that patient's condition. With such choice, he could feasibly choose a different drug each time, and always obtain the desired effect – (i.e. to reduce the patient's blood pressure, using a well tolerated drug). In effect, what this means to a doctor is that the 'risk' involved in not being loyal to one brand is very minimal, and *this* is actually the threat which **choices** create in pharmaceuticals.

So in theory, despite the millions which are spent testing, studying, developing and marketing a drug, you will often find that (as with so many other industries) the offer of product choice is a factor which threatens brand loyalty in any therapy area where such choices are available.

BAD PRESS FOR DRUGS

We have already discussed the impact which both the medical press and the tabloid press can have on *positively* generating interest in a drug – (i.e. through medical journals, newspapers and the internet). Conversely however, these same mediums are also able to generate *negative* emphasis for drugs which can similarly affect sales and uptake.

Over the years, there have been some very well documented drug withdrawals from the market– two of which have been in the last five years ('Lipobay' from Bayer, and 'Vioxx' from Merck Sharpe and Dohme). In both of these recent cases, the drugs in question were shown to increase mortality (i.e. risk of death) when used in particular clinical circumstances – despite them actually improving the conditions which they were indicated to treat.

In each case, the respective drug makers looked at the clinical and observational evidence which showed these risks, and then had little choice but to voluntarily withdraw these drugs from the market. In these types of circumstance it could hardly be said that 'bad press' affected their sales, since really they would have had no choice but to stop the drugs once such evidence came to light.

What *does* happen from occurrences like this however, are TWO negative consequential effects:

1. Doctors will subsequently become more concerned about the safety of *other* drugs in that same class
2. Doctors will inherently be apprehensive about *any* new product launches in general, since they will perceive there to *always* be a safety risk which can only be alleviated through the demonstration of safe administration to patients over a number of years.

Under the sub-heading of competitors above, I mentioned the fact that many doctors regard products which belong to one drug class as being similar and sometimes indistinguishable. Therefore in terms of clinicians' fears with regards to point 1 above, apart from the *genuine* possibility of such fatal drug effects being class-linked, it is clear that the *PERCEPTIONS* of drug similarities will amplify this fear in the minds of prescribers.

In terms of point 2, past years have seen many doctors take the view that *any* new drug is at least worth 'trying out' to assess its potential benefit to their patients. Now however, due to such bad press around medicines *generally*, you will see that many doctors will throw caution to the wind when it comes to using new drugs of *any* kind. You may quite often find them saying "*I will wait until my hospital gives me the go-ahead to use it"*, or *"I will wait a few years until the drug becomes established before I try it myself".*

Their argument is that if there are already a number of established alternatives that are already available within a particular market, then why would they want to take the risk of trying new drugs which are relatively untested? The threat of bad press within a market could therefore have a major impact on those companies who are launching new medications – especially if they are launching into established markets with reputable alternatives. Despite this, there could *still* be significant potential in new products which genuinely *do* serve unmet patient needs.

PARALLEL IMPORTS

Parallel imports (or Pis) are packs of branded medicines which have been produced overseas and then shipped inland to be dispensed in local pharmacies. These imports will usually have been produced by *your own* company for use in overseas markets, but will then have been discovered by local pharmacists at prices which are much cheaper than those offered by your company in *this* country.

This is a peculiar situation because logic would suggest that it should be cheapest for a pharmacist to purchase a product in the country in which it has been produced, rather than to purchase this same product from overseas. However due to influencing factors such as governmental pricing policies, import-export legislation and differentials in production costs, pharmacists are regularly able to buy in overseas drug stocks at lower prices. Because retail pharmacists are then reimbursed at UK tariff prices for the drugs they dispense, they stand to enjoy greater profits from obtaining these drugs at lower wholesale prices.

Such practice is entirely legitimate and can therefore be considered as a legal loophole in the system which pharmacists have learnt to take advantage of.

In 2002 it was estimated that 13% of all UK pharmaceutical sales were made up of parallel imports, which means that the UK has the largest proportion of parallel pharmaceutical trade in the *whole* of Europe[12].

Back in chapter 3 I described how a medical representative's sales are tracked. As discussed, their sales will ultimately be recognised by *pharmacy pack orders*, rather than by *GP scripts*.
Consider the following scenario;

A local GP is writing a vast number of prescriptions for your drug, but these are dispensed by a pharmacist who is obtaining Pis. You are unlikely to be credited for this increased prescribing, since RSA sales data does not include all PI stock. This is despite the fact that demand for those packs will have been directly driven by your activities,

What this demonstrates is that Pis can represent a significant threat to your business, or at least the business for which you are recognised.

Parallel imports cause a huge problem for the pharmaceutical industry when multinational drug makers are trying to track their sales independently from neighbouring countries. The irony is that no law exists to counteract this practice because parallel imports actually compliment the spirit of the European Union – i.e. to encourage free trade of goods between member states.

---

[12] 'Wellard's Guide to the NHS and Medicines' 2002 – Peter Merry.

What ends up happening therefore, is that pharmaceutical companies work hard to build up local markets, only to see the rewards invisibly pass them by, because ample volumes of these parallel stocks are being stacked on the shelves of local pharmacies. Unfortunately nothing can definitively be done to ensure that this stock is recognised as genuine, locally earned sales.

We work in an industry which has *so many* other complexities to overcome in order to recognise success – therefore seeing sales lost in this way can be bitterly disappointing. I myself have experienced such practice over the years, and it can be soul destroying to 'lose' business in this way. A metaphor which may describe this situation is to liken it to a home appliance salesperson. They may spend hours with a customer – going through product details, building a relationship and informing the customer on exact product specifications – only to see that customer subsequently purchase the product from an online retailer at a lower price.

Another irony in parallel imports is that GPs never have any deliberate intention of issuing Pis to their patients – in fact they are probably unaware of the origin of the drug which is being dispensed. In reality, they wouldn't have any reason to be concerned by this, just so long as the molecule that is being given to patients has identical clinical properties to that of the UK version of the drug (which of course Pis *do*). In this way, one can see that GPs cannot *really* influence the use of Pis. Ultimately therefore, the buck really does stop with the pharmacist.

At the time of going to print, the New Community Pharmacy Contract had not been fully implemented, though its introduction does offer the potential to minimise, if not fully remove the threat from Pis. The reason for this is quite complex, but in simple terms, the argument is as follows;

Since the NHS are trying to improve public health and patient care through a variety of stakeholders, they have stated that they will cut drug tariff prices on a number of branded medicines. With this money that will be saved on drug bills, they would theoretically redirect these funds into incentivising pharmacists (through the various patient services which were described in chapter 16). This would mean that the extra drug reimbursements which pharmacists could claim would be eroded. Therefore in many instances, this fall in tariff price would mean that it would make no difference to a pharmacist if they ordered UK, or imported stock.

So whilst the phenomenon of parallel trade definitely *is* a current threat to every representatives' business, the advent of the New Community Pharmacy Contract could potentially eliminate this problem. It remains to be seen however, how much effect this really will have on this current issue in pharmaceuticals.

Apart from this, the only other possible lifeline to alleviate this problem is that some companies are now buying in their sales monitoring data from third parties in such formats which actually *do* recognise PI stock as being locally generated sales. The way this works is that if pharmacists are ordering their PI stock from the larger reputable wholesalers, then PI stocks are still able to be included in sales volume measures. If however, other pharmacists *still* choose to source their PI stock from small independent wholesalers, this stock is again likely to be omitted from final sales measures.

TIME LAG IN SALES DATA

Again, this issue was discussed in chapter 3, but it is worth highlighting again because although you would probably not describe this factor as being an actual threat to your business within itself, the time lag in receiving sales data creates the artificial obstacle of having to work 6-8 weeks behind 'real time'.

Therefore what could potentially happen, is that (for example) a significant market change may occur in a given month, but because you are now past that actual time, you cannot do anything to address the problem – it will simply appear as a sudden blip on your sales data once it is published. This could result in a competitor being able to take a stronghold in a local market without being competitively challenged, for example. The issue of data time lag, is therefore an important consideration to make when business planning in pharmaceuticals.

CLINICIAN'S MEMORY/RECALL

This threat simply refers to those customers who may be completely convinced about your product's benefits and have every intention of prescribing it, but due to various pressures, forget to *actually* prescribe your drug when relevant patients present to them in their clinics. They would instead automatically revert to prescribing whatever they have done previously – i.e. a competitor product, or an older style treatment.

Whilst I have listed this factor as a threat, I must also say that consequently, if this barrier is overcome, then it can actually become a powerful force for long term *protection* of your business too. What I mean is that if for example, you can kick-start a customer to initiate your product on just a few occasions, they may well begin to use *your* product habitually, which obviously is the ultimate achievement in this job. This 'habit' will then effectively create a barrier which protects the use of your drug from that of a *competitors,* as it is then *your* product which 'automatically' comes to the clinician's mind – thereby resulting in the competitor having to work to overcome the habitual prescribing of *your* drug.

I can recall many occasions when I have delivered multiple sales calls over a period of months with the same customer – each time they have said all the right things, but due to a lack of mental recall at the time of prescribing, they had always forgotten to initiate my product when a relevant patient presented. Despite this, when they *did* eventually manage to start 1-2 patients on the product, a virtual snowballing effect was created. What I mean by this is that it was almost as if the act of prescribing the drug on a trial basis was enough to imprint it in their minds to a point where they would then recall my product *every time* they saw a patient who fitted the required profile for my drug.

As a result of such habitual prescribing, I have regularly heard customers jovially using phrases such as 'once the hand starts, it just writes the product by itself!'. As I have said, once you can progress a customer to this stage, then you really are onto a winner as you will have achieved your ultimate aim.

THE NUMBER OF INFLUENCING FACTORS ON PRESCRIBING

Many optimists would argue that this is actually an opportunity rather than a threat to your business, since more factors could mean more opportunity to influence. I would agree to a certain extent, but as I have already suggested in previous chapters, the number of influencing factors in pharmaceutical prescribing are so varied that I would challenge *anyone* to be able to *definitively* isolate *which* of the influencing factors are *most* powerful. It is this inability to suggest what it is that actually works, that makes this factor a threat.

Imagine (as is often the case) that you have a limited budget with which to raise your product's market share. How do you go about it? Which influencing factor/'s would you invest your resource in – advertising, clinical trials, national meetings, sales representatives? And if you *do* choose to invest in sales representatives, then which groups should they focus on? GPs, hospitals or PCTs?

These questions can be endless, and I argue that nobody can definitively suggest which solution is best since no-one *really* knows *exactly* where the biggest 'bang-per-buck' actually lies. This is why I conclude that the inability to highlight exact influences on prescribing presents a threat to your work as a medical representative.

PART 3

PUTTING IT ALL TOGETHER – YOUR FIRST THREE MONTHS ON TERRITORY

18. SEGMENTATION AND GP TARGET LISTS

Many years ago medical representatives were universally tasked with seeing and influencing *all* GPs who practiced within their geographical sales territories. Whilst this was an effective strategy at the time, most pharmaceutical companies are now more conscious of where they place the resource of medical representatives – mainly because they come at a significant expense to the organisation.

Therefore companies now believe that if they are financing the work of representatives, then they should be directed towards those prescribers who are more likely to prescribe their promoted brands. In this way representatives will be smarter and more focussed about how and where they focus their efforts rather than the old 'blanket' method of selling.

Target lists can therefore simply be defined as lists of doctors who have been profiled to indicate those who are more likely to prescribe your drug. This greater likelihood to prescribe a particular drug may be determined by a number of qualifying factors such as;

- Does the GP have a particular clinical interest, and is therefore more likely to see the type of illnesses which your drug treats?
- Does the GP work in a large practice where they are more likely to have your target patient types referred to them by other GPs in the practice?
- Does the GP have a known preference to prescribe your *class* of drug?
- Does the GP practice in a part of the country which is more predisposed to serving patients of a particular clinical category – e.g. elderly patients, or diabetics?

These would be the *kinds* of questions that would be considered when determining which GPs are likely to be of a higher 'value' to representatives. It is however, the job of the marketing department either to carry out such market research themselves, or to outsource this task to an external agency.

What definitely IS in your remit however, is the requirement to spend virtually *all* of your efforts, energy and resources in working towards developing *these* doctors as your main target customer base.

I would therefore recommend that even *before* you finish your training course, one of the first things you should do is to speak to your area manager to obtain a current target list for your sales territory. By doing this it will allow you to forward plan and make appointments with these key customers in preparation for your first few weeks out on territory.

Target lists tend to form the very hub of your day to day work on territory, and so are very important documents. For this reason I believe it is worth pointing out to readers that there are some difficulties surrounding the issue of target list development. Simply put, due to the confidentiality afforded to clinical prescribing, the pharmaceutical industry will never have full access to individual doctor prescribing – therefore the segmentation and profiling which is carried out, is based on the discretion of those doctors who are happy to divulge their prescribing habits during voluntary market research.

For this reason I believe that it is important to appreciate that there may be some prescribers who choose not to take part in such research, and may therefore not be profiled as being of a high value (*not to say that they aren't of a high prescribing value*). Because of this, it is important for companies to allow sales representatives to spend an agreed amount of their activity and resources on non-segmented or 'non-target' customers in addition to the target customers. This ensures that representatives can use their individual judgement to establish which of the non-target customers may be of a greater value.

When all is said and done regarding these minor anomalies however, readers should make no mistake that companies will be very focussed on their targeting campaigns year on year. This will mean that the volume of activity spent on target customers will *always* be a key measure of success in annual appraisals for medical representatives.

19. DEVELOPING ACCESS INFORMATION

Access information is simply a list of ideal times and days when each GP on a given sales territory will prefer to accommodate sales representatives' visits. Developing GP access information is fundamental to the role of a medical representative, yet I am still surprised by how many representatives choose to keep this bank of information in the repositories of their mind! The reason why this occurs is that GP access information is invariably referred to on a daily basis in this role – what tends to happen therefore, is that representatives start to habitually memorise access times, and therefore the temptation is to stop recording such information once you believe you are able to remember most of it.

I accept that access information can change very quickly, but in an industry where primary care sales teams are so often made up of more than one representative, I believe it is far more useful to make this information accessible and transparent – either through writing it down, or by recording it electronically. This can be done using electronic spreadsheets, or can even be recorded in some ETMS systems (also see next chapter).

Ideally, I would recommend that *any* basic access information should contain the following information as a minimum standard (most of this should be obtainable in the duration of a phone call);

- *Preferred day* of the week when the doctor likes to see representatives
- *Preferred time* when doctor likes to see representatives
- Whether these visits should be by pre-arranged *appointments or 'spec'-calls'*
- Do the practice take bookings for representative lunch meetings? If so, on which days/times?

- Any other general information which is needed to aid access (e.g. is there a particular secretary who deals with appointment bookings).

As mentioned, the easiest way to obtain this information is generally to telephone each surgery individually and simply ask the reception staff. YES! This can be a long, painstaking task, but since this information will guide every working day in your role, it is well worth investing in properly when you are starting out.

If the above information *is* recorded as advised above, then this can be shared with relevant team colleagues as appropriate, and of course when you eventually do move on into your *own* next career move, this information will support the *next* person who takes up your position – therefore saving them from having to *'reinvent the wheel'*, and re-do the entire task again.

20. USING AND DEVELOPING YOUR ETMS SYSTEM

The majority of companies nowadays subscribe to an Electronic Territory Management System (or ETMS). This is simply a powerful electronic database containing a full list of every healthcare professional who works within your geographical territory (GPs, nurses, practice managers, health visitors, hospital doctors, and sometimes PCT managers and staff).

The idea of such systems is that they store large amounts of information about these customers such as their main working locations, addresses, phone numbers and so forth. In addition however, this database will be the central place from which all customer contacts will be recorded by yourself and your team colleagues. That is, each time a customer is seen, a contact will need to be recorded into their 'file'. The things that will need to be highlighted in such records will be the *date* of the contact, the *type* of contact made (i.e. meeting/face to face call) and most importantly a short set of notes outlining a synopsis of the discussion that took place between you and the customer.

Again, I will not give guidance on how exactly this should be recorded, since each company will have their own preference for how they want this to be done. What I *will* say though, is that this is *another* key area where many representatives have traditionally been very slack. It becomes all too easy to simply record a contact for the sake of logging in your activities for the day, without actually taking the time to highlight what it is that you discussed with the customer, and therefore how it was received by them. The benefit of doing this efficiently would be that when you or a colleague came around to seeing that customer the next time, the call notes will help you to recall both the major outcomes, *and* the minor details of the discussion. This information will then help you (or your colleague) to prepare appropriately and follow up the next call with the customer.

Using a disciplined system of call recording and call planning in this way can really enhance your interactions with your customers, since the process can be used to monitor progress with all target GPs on an individual basis. In the absence of such a process, it will be very difficult to establish any continuity and progress through your calls, since quite simply, you would probably not even be able to remember what you discussed with them the last time!

Just as with the example of access information given in the previous chapter, it would also be a 'missed opportunity' if you were not to diligently record call notes through your ETMS system. By doing this properly, both current colleagues AND new colleagues can view call histories to be able to establish how a customer has (or has not) been developed. Such historical information is vital to know when you are working with customers over the long term to try and influence their prescribing.

As mentioned, ETMS systems are powerful tools which can store vast amounts of customer intelligence. As a tie-in with the last section on access information therefore, you will no doubt be made aware that some ETMS systems will actually allow access information to be recorded within the customer database itself. This can be very useful since it will mean that *all* information pertaining to individual customers could be stored in just one database, making it easier to access quickly.

Under the heading of ETMS systems it is also worth noting that the long term vision for most organisations is for their ETMS systems to be used to implement true Customer Relationship Management, or 'CRM'. This concept suggests that all business related information known about customers should be recorded and stored in the relevant sections of the ETMS so that ultimately, companies will actually be able to segment their customer base by using the information held within the companies' own computer database. It should be noted however, that restrictions relating to the Data Protection Act will apply to the use of such information. Therefore *personal* customer information is never allowed to be recorded on such systems and any other types of information are not necessarily available to be passed freely around the business.

For example, if a company were preparing to launch a new drug, then they could simply run systematic searches of their ETMS database to determine which customers have a key interest in that clinical area. Or if a company announced results of a new clinical study, then they could use the system to assess which customers have historically taken a keen interest in clinical trial information, and would therefore possibly be more receptive to being made aware of new trial data.

If companies will implement such processes, then the benefit *to their customers* would be that such targeted approaches would be far more timely and relevant to individual clinicians, rather than mass mailings or vast numbers of contacts being made to random customers who may have no real interest in what is being discussed.

As discussed, most ETMS systems have the *potential* to be able to store this amount of customer knowledge. In my own opinion however, the real potential for these systems will only ever be realised if associates from *all* levels of a company utilise them appropriately and consistently. This would mean that *all* associates from organisational departments such as sales, marketing or medical information *must* use the ETMS system to record *any* professional information which is collated about customers. Until this happens, I believe that most ETMS systems will continue to be underutilised.

21. MY GOLDEN PRINCIPLES FOR SUCCESS!

In chapter 13 I outlined the many factors which are thought to influence a doctor in prescribing a product. As already discussed, the reasons can be so varied and diverse, that in reality it is impossible to isolate the *exact* prescribing motivators for individual clinicians. Because of this, I would challenge *anyone* who believes they can write an *absolute* formula for success in pharmaceutical sales.

Despite this, there are undoubtedly *some* key principles which certainly can contribute towards maximising your chances of success. What I have done in this final chapter therefore, is to select some random success factors which are not only conducive to successful outcomes, but which also tend *not* to be covered in standard representative initial training programmes.

The first nine rules relate directly to your interactions with customers, whilst the remaining three rules give guidance on your self management within the role.

PRINCIPLE 1: REMEMBER THAT PEOPLE BUY PEOPLE

Once again, I will take this opportunity to remind you that I am only asserting my own opinion – not necessarily fact, but a strong belief of mine nonetheless.

The principle that 'people buy people' is a very well accepted concept in sales circles. To explain what we mean by this principle, the following example can be used;

> *If in any given sales situation two salespeople are selling the same product, WHY is it that as the consumer, I will consistently buy my product from 'Salesperson-A' rather than 'Salesperson-B'? According to the above theory, the answer would be*

*that I am actually 'buying-into' the person, before even considering the relative merits of the products. It could be Salesperson-A's professionalism, charm, personality, selling style or even their manner of speaking – in fact, the gravitation towards Salesperson-A is actually **anything** that that person does in order to successfully engage me as the customer.*

Regardless of what the scientific reason is, the 'people-buy-people' theory states that I as the consumer, will continually buy my product from Salesperson-A, despite the competing products being identical. In fact, the theory could even go so far as to say that if it were quite clearly proven that Salesperson-B's product were better, then my relationship with Salesperson-A will *still* keep me loyal to them. It could almost be described as a form of 'brand loyalty', whereby the 'brand' is actually the salesperson. Whatever it is, this intangible quality is something which *that* salesperson is able to replicate again and again in order to draw-in customers, and translate this into consistent sales success.

I have already discussed the fact that many competing products in pharmaceutical sales are broadly indistinguishable. There may be subtle differences in side effect profile, in evidence base or clinical indications, but essentially the efficacy of these drugs will be fairly similar. So if a GP were to think logically about which drug he should choose to prescribe, then all that should really matter is that:

- A drug should work adequately
- It should cause minimal side effects
- It should be competitively priced

Therefore in a market place where there are a number of such drugs in one therapeutic class which can apparently

ALL fit this criteria, which drug might the doctor choose? You've guessed it! The doctor will prescribe the drug which is promoted by the representative whom he most likes! Is this unethical or wrong on the part of the doctor? *ABSOLUTELY NOT!* Why would it be? After all, if the competing products perform as effectively as each other then the patients in question will not lose out in any way – therefore why should such practice be regarded as unethical?

This is why I firmly believe that the innate ability of a salesperson to be able to engage and build rapport with people is a vital key to sales success – particularly in undifferentiated markets such as those described above.

Prior to becoming a pharmaceutical sales professional, I (like I am sure many people looking at this industry do), used to think the selling function of a medical sales representative is intensely science-based. Do not get me wrong – with many customers this *will* still be the case, but if this measurable competency is synergised with the instinctive ability to build a unique rapport with customers, then this can be a powerful recipe for success in pharmaceutical sales. Why? Because the *people-buy-people* principle applies in *this* field just as much as in any other traditional selling role.

It is clear that pharmaceutical companies are highly proficient at equipping new salespeople with the relevant scientific knowledge required to sell their products. (*I myself*, was in fact a rookie with a totally non-scientific background when I first started!) Unfortunately however, there are no developmental courses which you can attend in order to become a better 'people-person' (not in pharmaceutical circles anyway!) Most courses which *are* available can at best, teach you principles to improve your general approach and develop your level of professionalism, but *no* course could ever *really* give you this 'gift' as it is something which is intrinsic.

So what does this mean for you? Well, if in a past guise (sales or otherwise) you have unexplainably been a person who can strike up an instant rapport with people from all walks of life, then you may well have that inherent 'X-factor' which (if superimposed with the thorough scientific armoury you will need for this job), *could* mean that you will be an *exceptional* pharmaceutical sales representative.

PRINCIPLE 2: HONOUR CUSTOMER REQUESTS

This is perhaps an obvious point for any business person who is in a customer facing role, yet I am still surprised to see how often this is overlooked by so many representatives.

It is vital to maintain your professional integrity by ensuring that you follow up those customer requests which you are able to serve (e.g. requests for items or clinical information). I am amazed at how often customers question if I will *actually* honour the promises which I make them, since they have a perception that medical representatives are notorious for not keeping to their word – even with the simplest of requests. I would suggest that all representatives should therefore use this scepticism to their advantage, and be sure to be seen as one of the 'good guys' in the eyes of their customers.

What I mean by this, is that if the automatic perception is that we are *all* unreliable, then by doing the exact opposite and sticking to your word, you will easily be able to carve out a niche for yourself as one of the 'reliable few!' It is also useful to remember once again that technically, no doctor is obliged to see you in your role as medical representative. It is therefore imperative that you respect their time and their wishes once you *do* manage to see them!

PRINCIPLE 3: DO NOT BE DISPARAGING ABOUT YOUR COMPETITORS

Apart from actually being a rule of the ABPI, there are many doctors who find this approach to our job extremely off-putting and sometimes even offensive. I am sure that if you were to ask *ANY* GP what are the three worst habits of bad representatives, then this one would always be up there!

I am not suggesting that you completely avoid making comparisons with your competitor products, but merely that this should be done in a way which is professional, constructive and justifiable. Being dismissive of competitors can come across as unprofessional and unpleasant. In an industry where clinical evidence counts for so much, there will always be a way of constructing an intellectual and evidence based argument as to why *your* product should preferentially be prescribed over your competitor's product.

However, if you find there ISN'T any credible data with which to do displace your competitors, then don't even try to do so. Instead, it would be best to avoid comparisons by simply emphasising the merits of your own product. It is far more beneficial for you to maintain your professional respect and credibility, rather than risking it for the sake of a cheap dig at a competitor – I can promise you that customers will not appreciate this.

PRINCIPLE 4: AIM TO BE THE EXPERT IN YOUR PRODUCT AND THERAPY AREA

When I was interviewed for my hospital specialist role, I was asked if I felt I had the confidence to challenge senior hospital doctors on their prescribing habits. At this stage of my career I had been selling the drug in question for a number of years already, so I was fairly comfortable with my level of knowledge around it. I did however make it my mission to sharpen up my clinical knowledge even further – not only for my own product, but for my competitor products. Armed with this holistic expertise, I was confident that I could construct a convincing argument to challenge *any* customer's thinking. In short, I firmly believe in the old adage that *knowledge is power* – in our case, I believe that knowledge gives us power to sell more effectively.

As a consumer myself, I have been subject to some expert selling by many strong salespeople in the past (from *all* kinds of industries). The common skills which these people all demonstrated were:

- Excellent knowledge of their *own* product
- A comprehensive knowledge of *their* competitor's products
- And a thorough understanding of the overall context in which these products were used

Combining these three elements, they were consistently able to present compelling arguments from *every* perspective – yet this was not done in an over-zealous manner. As a buyer it actually gave me more confidence in what I was purchasing. I really felt that buying from these salespeople meant that I was making informed choices.

It is therefore my firm belief that the flawless execution of selling skills *alone* will not make you a good salesperson. You must *also* have the clinical/background knowledge alongside which such techniques should be applied.

Ultimately, if I had to choose between a salesperson who had good selling skills but limited clinical knowledge, versus someone who had unmatched product and therapy area knowledge but average selling skills, I would certainly choose the latter – i.e. the knowledge expert.

PRINCIPLE 5: BE IN THE RELATIONSHIP FOR THE LONG TERM

Every pharmaceutical company will stipulate that target customers should be seen sequentially (either through meetings or face to face calls). In an environment where relationships can count for so much, my advice would therefore be to contribute a proportion of these calls to actually 'marketing yourself'. Really, this goes back to the people-buy-people principle.

I am not suggesting that this is spent as 'social time', but certainly the aim should be to establish some common ground with the customer in order to try and build an individual relationship. There is no fixed formula on how to do this, but suffice to say that this will entail doing *ANYTHING BUT* giving them the endless 'hard-sell'!

If you use your intuitive, natural style with your customers in this way, I can assure you this will pay dividends since customers will begin to view you as a more friendly, more likeable representative! – not a 'Robo-Rep' who has been designed to bombard them with finely rehearsed marketing messages each time you see them! Remember, that the sales process in pharmaceuticals is very much a marathon and not a sprint, so be in the relationship for the long term.

PRINCIPLE 6: ALWAYS ENSURE YOUR CUSTOMERS ASSOCIATE YOU WITH YOUR PRODUCT

On face value, this heading could look like a contradiction of the last one! – in actual fact, what this is, is a reality check that will stop you from taking the previous rule too far. In using your rapport building skills to move away from the 'robot-salesperson' approach, it is vital that you should not make the mistake of veering right over to the other extreme – that is, the *'loveable, friendly representative whose products are never discussed or remembered by the prescribers!'*

Traditionally, those doctors who routinely see representatives will have come across three types;

- Those who 'sell to the death' in *every call* (affectionately known by GPs as the *'nightmare reps!'*)
- Those who do not discuss their product at all and simply believe that spending time building a relationship will result in automatic sales
- The final type being the representative who strikes a fine balance between the 'rapport' and 'business' elements of a call. These representatives are welcomed by customers due to their personable approach, but they are also consistently associated with their products

Over the years I can recall countless instances when doctors have struggled to remember my name, but they have simply referred to me as the "Product-X" representative. Although they sometimes feel quite awkward about this, I actually take it as a huge compliment, because the instantaneous recall of my product affirms to me that I must be doing the most important part of my job effectively!

It is also worth mentioning a scenario which may occasionally be encountered – this is the GP who agrees to see a representative, but who is not in the mood to discuss products. As I outlined back in chapter 5, one of the many reasons why a doctor may agree to see you is to receive some 'light relief' from seeing demanding patients during a busy clinic. In such a scenario many customers will let their guard down so much with representatives, that *all* they will want to do is have a good old chat, with no business on the agenda!

I would suggest that by all means, *do* allow them to do this as they will appreciate the respite from their often hectic patient interactions. For your sake however, do not make the mistake of ending such calls without a discussion about your products.

We need to be assertive enough, and *principled* enough to ensure that some substantive dialogue relating to our products is *always* exchanged in any interaction with a doctor.

The really successful representatives are the ones who can understand these concepts and find a good balance between rapport building and ensuring that customers are maintaining a constant association with their promoted products.

PRINCIPLE 7: UNDERSTAND THE DYNAMICS BEHIND 'CLOSING' A SALE

This is an interesting point which relates directly to our job purpose, and specifically to the topical, yet delicate issue of sales closing in pharmaceuticals. The reason why it is *topical*, is that many people truly believe that pharmaceutical sales growth could be enhanced by consistent sales closing. The reason why this issue is *delicate* however, is that if asked, I would imagine that the vast majority of customers would probably not see sales closing as a conducive way to conclude a sales call as they often find this quite threatening.

Therefore, there are three key learning points to note under this heading.

1. Remember, that as medical representatives we are employed to increase clinicians' prescribing of our products which invariably means *changing* prescribing habits. As part of your standard sales training it is likely that you will be taught to probe customers down a route which presents them with a potential need. Your product will then be positioned to meet that need. As part of this training therefore, you will always be taught to close a sale and ask for commitment to prescribe once you have completed this process.

I believe however that to ask a customer to *directly* and *immediately* commit to *your* suggested course of action, could result in them perceiving that you are asking for too much in one call and have possibly been too pushy, too soon – therefore this is NOT always appropriate. Instead, a good tactic is to simply ask customers what *their* opinion is of the arguments you have put forward – if they agree with them, then you have succeeded in your goal of influencing them; if they *disagree* with your arguments, then this will indicate to you that more work needs to be done in subsequent calls before a commitment is agreed.

It is clear that aggressive sales closing can be an *ineffective* means to influencing prescribing behaviour because of the simple fact that managing *any* type of change clearly takes time.

Think about the last time you were required to change something which you had been used to for a long time.

Could you have *instantly* committed to a permanent change just because someone gave you a reason to? Probably not. Why? Because human behaviour dictates that mindset changes cannot always be instantaneous. Therefore in the context of pharmaceuticals, I believe that medical representatives need to appreciate that wholesale prescribing changes cannot be made during the course of one sales call.

I know of a GP in London who was happy to see medical representatives, and who found the interactions with them to be very useful. He was however, regularly disappointed by representatives who would present extremely strong and diligent clinical arguments, then go in for a 'hard sales close' – he felt that doing this actually devalued the substance of the entire preceding conversation.

In summary therefore, my first rule of sales closing is to remember that **'managing change takes time'**.

2. Secondly I believe that sales closing in pharmaceuticals does not always have to be an agreement to change prescribing habit, but can constitute an agreement of some other kind – a process that I refer to as partial or intermediate-closing.

So if you felt that asking for a *permanent change* in prescribing behaviour was too much to do in one sales call, then an intermediate commitment could be focussed on instead – perhaps something just as simple as asking the customer to read through some clinical evidence to back up your argument. By doing this for example, the customer would also have time to become used to the idea of what you are proposing, and perhaps not feel so threatened and overawed by it. Therefore rule number two is to **'use an *appropriate* close'**.

3. Finally, I have found over the years that if you can put forward a good enough argument as to why a customer should change their prescribing habit, then the weight of the argument itself can be enough to convince them to change.

I can recall numerous occasions in past sales calls when I had some extremely lengthy clinical debates with customers. I would nonetheless come out of such calls feeling as if I had reached a stalemate with them. However, in subsequent visits it became apparent that these customers had actually taken on board my arguments from previous discussions, and tried prescribing my products based on the reasoning which I proposed.

This has lead me to the belief that people do not always like to admit that their current ways of practising could be improved upon, but if you cannot make them commit to change verbally, then you *MUST* at least make your arguments thought-provoking enough to *invite a* change. Therefore rule number three is to **'ensure your clinical arguments are compelling enough to encourage change'**.

Also, it would not be over-dramatic to suggest that hard-sales tactics fail on not just one, but two key points;

- Firstly, they do not always yield the desired outcome in the immediacy
- Secondly such methods can even result in doctors refusing you subsequent access to them, for fear that they will be subjected to similarly uncomfortable pressure each time they see you. As I discussed in chapter 5, our industry is unique in that a customer (i.e. a doctor) can readily use the products produced by pharmaceutical companies without ever really having to liaise with a

salesperson of any kind. Therefore the threat of customers refusing to see you is very real, and must be carefully managed.

I can recall a few years back when I bought an investment property in London. It was a newly built apartment which was being sold by a property development company. The sales office was fronted by a proverbial *'nightmare salesperson'* – he was unprofessional, unhelpful and generally disorganised. I cringed at the thought of having to liaise with him to have to purchase my new property, but the fact was that I actually *had to* work with him as he was the only person who looked after my site! In this situation, I had no choice.

The interesting choice which doctors *do* have however, is that they do not have to entertain representative sales calls in order to have access to our products, and it is for this reason that I see it as critical that we strike a fine balance between meeting our commercial objectives, whilst maintaining the delicate equilibrium of a good customer relationship. Ultimately it is this, that will guarantee us regular access to our prescribers, and therefore the platform on which to be able to increase our sales.

PRINCIPLE 8: EVERY CUSTOMER IS DIFFERENT – NEVER ASSUME, AND ALWAYS BE CURIOUS

This is actually a generic rule of selling, but again is particularly pertinent to *pharmaceutical* sales. You will find in this job, that it becomes very easy to generalise about customers – in terms of their professional concerns, their practice habits and most of all their *prescribing* habits. I urge you however, *never* to take any of this for granted, since a lack of curiosity about your customers will result in you missing out on discovering key individualities about them, which would otherwise help you to sell more relevantly to them as individuals in the long run.

In order to help you discover these unique customer traits, I will pass on some advice which I learnt from an excellent sales coach of mine. She always said that one must always be *genuinely curious* when learning about customers. This doesn't just mean asking 'off-the-shelf', standardised sales probes to customers when in call, but it actually means that one should adopt a *genuine* curiosity about their needs, opinions, backgrounds and circumstances. If you can understand this difference in approach, you will find that you will not only ask *more* questions, but you will also ask *more useful* questions. Such questions will provide you with the type of information which you can then use to build more individualised profiles for your key customers.

Another major benefit of using this technique is that you will learn so much more about the job itself. Throughout my 'training room' learnings in this industry, I have always sought to verify what I have learnt in theory, with how my customers see these subjects in reality. This has always allowed me to see varied opinions about key subjects, but in an ironic way it has also endeared my customers towards me since they have always welcomed my curiosity.

Why was this? Well it was quite simply because I was always curious about the subjects which *they* knew *all* about. Think about it – when was the last time someone wanted *you* to explain something to them which you knew *all* about? Were you not more than happy to share your wisdom with them? Of course you were! People inherently love to express their own opinions on issues which they know about – especially when it is about themselves! This makes them feel that their opinions are both utilised and valued, so it always pays to be curious!

PRINCIPLE 9: ALWAYS HAVE A TANGIBLE REASON TO SEE YOUR CUSTOMERS – MAINTAIN CALL BRIDGING

The concept of call bridging can simply be defined as establishing a clear reason for making a follow up call on a customer. Call bridging can therefore be as complex as making a commitment with a customer to organise a local consultant meeting, yet it can also be as simple as agreeing with a customer to come back and discuss how your drug has performed in a particular patient.

There are two simple reasons why it is important to implement this principle;

1. Firstly, if you have a tangible reason to return to a customer then they will quite simply, be more likely to see you.
2. Secondly, call bridging helps you to maintain a consistent frequency of visits where regular access to a customer may otherwise be difficult.

In addition to the methods mentioned above, another strategy is to utilise reply paid card (RPC) programmes. The concept of RPC programmes is where your marketing team will conduct a centralised mailing to key customers offering a clinical item or inexpensive gift. Customers who choose to receive the item will be asked to indicate which day and time they may be willing to accommodate a representative visit on, in order to have the item delivered personally by a representative.

It should be noted however, that as an ABPI rule, if a customer chooses to receive the item but *not* see a representative, then you are absolutely obliged to leave the item behind without meeting with the customer. In reality however, I have always found that unless you are perceived as a 'nightmare rep' by your customers, it is quite unlikely that a GP will take an item without doing you the honour of sparing you at least a few minutes to discuss your products!

Other ways to create call bridging are to simply gain *verbal* commitment by asking for 'permission' to return in order to have some sort of follow up discussion – for example to gain feedback after a speaker meeting. As mentioned previously, the use of value added services (such as auditing and general support services) are also an excellent way to bridge calls and to demonstrate your professional support for customers. I would urge any new representative to take some time to understand what tools are at your disposal in order to help implement this principle.

PRINCIPLE 10: TAKE CONTROL OF YOUR OWN LEARNING, AND USE THE SUPPORT OFFERED BY YOUR COMPANY

The internal company network of support which tends to be offered to new representatives is excellent. It is both varied in terms of *who* can support you, yet is always thorough and comprehensive too. In their early careers, new representatives can expect to be offered the combined support of *head office* trainers, *field* trainers, nominated mentors, peer colleagues and of course area managers. It would be foolish not to utilise this support, as so much can be learnt so quickly from these people around you. Remember, at some point in *their* careers, they will *all* have been where you are now, so it makes sense to learn from them.

One of my area managers knew that before each day she spent out with me, I would always have a list of random questions about the job which I would have been pondering over! The beauty was that I could ask her *anything* about the role that didn't make sense to me, and she was always more than willing to answer these questions herself (if she could do so), or to pass me on to someone who *could* answer the question if she couldn't!

The need to manage one's own learning was again reaffirmed as an important success factor during my leadership training programme a few years ago, where *'self managed development'* was firmly encouraged. As I have said, you will always be offered a strong network of support, but if you can proactively take control of your own learning to *utilise* this network, you will accelerate your development to become much more *effective* much more *quickly*.

PRINCIPLE 11: ALWAYS UPDATE YOUR BRAG FILE

A brag file is simply a folder containing evidence of your key achievements throughout your career. It can consist of certificates, memos, e-mails, league tables – basically *anything* which tangibly highlights the successes which you have achieved in your work. A brag file will be an invaluable tool in supporting you for two key things – year-end performance appraisals, and future career moves. *Both* these situations will command evidence of work successes which is why brag files are invaluable.

This industry is extremely fast moving and it is amazing how small successes can easily pass you by unless you capture these high points as and when they happen.

PRINCIPLE 12: BE A SALESPERSON – NOT A NUMBER CRUNCHER

Representatives will generally be asked to meet a minimum volume of daily customer contacts – a concept known as a 'call rate'. The exact requirements may vary from one company to the next, because different geographical areas will have differing levels of accessibility – but basically, the more accessible a territory is, the higher your call rate target will be.

One of the questions that new representatives will eventually find themselves asking therefore, is *why exactly* do these call rates exist? Ultimately, sales managers believe that setting call rates targets will guide representatives towards seeing a sufficient number of prescribers in order to generate necessary sales revenues.

The best metaphor I can use to describe this is a footballing one!

> *If SALES is likened to scoring goals, then CALL RATES correlate to how many shots you get on target – therefore the more shots you get on target, the more goals you are likely to score. After all, how can you score goals if you are shooting off target?! The issue perhaps, is that if a football team never scored any goals but had hundreds of shots on target, then the end result would still be the same – NO GOALS i.e. NO SALES!*

This is why it is important to put call rates into context, and recognise that they are definitely just a surrogate measure – certainly not a success factor in their own right.

The anomaly of call rates however, is that many representatives find them to be stretching and sometimes even distracting. A number of representatives feel that on a day to day basis, the need to balance the two primary objectives of increasing sales whilst maintaining high call rates can sometimes only be achieved at the expense of letting one or the other slip. Imagine the following example:

You find yourself locked in a lengthy, intense discussion with one customer where you really feel that you are on your way to securing some business. On the other hand, you have one eye on the clock knowing that you are getting late for your next appointment – one where you stand to see two more customers at once (meaning that you will have then seen your target rate of 3 GPs for the day). So now you must make a choice: whether to stay put and make sure you properly conclude the current discussion, or to cut the conversation short in an attempt to ensure that you meet your call rate target for the day by realising your next appointment.

My only plea to you from a *sales* viewpoint, is that in deciding how to manage this challenge, PLEASE do not ever lose sight of the *primary* objective of your job – which is definitely to *increase sales* for your promoted products.

Call rates will only ever be a means to an end – just a vehicle towards increasing sales. Having a high call rate does not guarantee you a sale – it only puts you in front of a customer – *what you actually do in front of that customer* is a whole different thing. My own personal fear for the job is that if too much emphasis is placed on call rates over the long term, then we will become 'number-crunchers' rather than salespeople – this would be unforgivable.

Call rates are a necessary marker that will not go away and the best that representatives can do is to accept this. It should also be noted that call rates now tend to form a considerable proportion of annual appraisal ratings in most companies – so achieving them plays a part in your overall success.

In short, my advice is to strive to achieve the call rates because they won't go away, but never do so at the expense of effective, persuasive selling.

A FINAL WORD..........

As I said right at the top of this book, I have always found this industry to be dynamic, exciting, challenging and rewarding.

I hope this book has given you enough – either to inspire you to make that first application, *or* to support you in your first months as a new medical sales representative. Either way I trust that reading this book will turn out to be an important and rewarding step towards what will be a most successful pharmaceutical sales career for you.

Happy Selling!

Sahil Syed - Author

As this is *my* first book – and indeed one of the first of its kind in the UK, we are extremely keen to hear your thoughts about it....

Please email your comments, questions and feedback to:

Psfp.bookinfo@yahoo.co.uk

Please also email us at this address if you would like to purchase further copies

PART 4

APPENDIX

PHARMACEUTICAL RECRUITMENT
AGENCIES IN THE UK

The following are a list of recruitment agencies operating in the UK. They specialise in placing high calibre pharmaceutical sales candidates with leading pharmaceutical companies.

Pharmaceutical Sales for Phools has a direct link with GEM Resourcing. The director, **Niall Barry,** is a key industry expert who has critically reviewed and endorsed this book.

GEM RESOURCING
BioCentre
York Science Park
Heslington
York
YO10 5NY
01759 373 079
www.gem-resourcing.co.uk

Other pharmaceutical recruitment specialists in the UK include:

ADVANCE RECRUITMENT
0800 783 0920
www.advancerecruitment.net

ASHFIELD
0870 850 1234
www.ashfieldhealthcare.com

CHASE
0131 553 6644
www.chasepharmajobs.co.uk

FLAME
0800 0850858
www.flamepharma.com

FUTURES RESOURCING
01256 355955
www.futures-resourcing.com

IHS
0208 834 1024
www.i-hs.co.uk

IN2FOCUS
01628 488 606
www.in2focus.com

INNOVEX
01344 601550
www.innovexcareers.co.uk

INVENTIVE SOLUTIONS
0845 129 8582
www.inventive-solutions.co.uk

NORTH-51
0115 950 2500
www.north-51.com

PANMEDICA
01494 461 001
www.panmedica.co.uk

ROYCE CONSULTANCY
0208 972 8300
www.royceconsultancy.com

SEARCH
0207 929 3900
www.search.co.uk

STAR MEDICAL
0870 242 2025
www.starmedical.co.uk

THE VACANCY MANAGEMENT COMPANY
01420 82202
www.vacancymgt.com

ZENOPA
0870 220 4368
www.zenopa.com

SUMMARY OF ABBREVIATIONS AND TERMS
USED IN THIS BOOK

4S – 'Scandinavian Simvastatin Survival Study' (statin study carried out by Merck Sharpe and Dohme Pharmaceuticals)
ABPI – Association of British Pharmaceutical Industries - the representative body of the pharmaceutical industry in the UK

ASYMPTOMATIC – Describes an illness in which a patient may not experience any symptoms, despite the definite presence of a condition

BMJ – British Medical Journal – A clinical journal read by many healthcare professionals in the UK

BNF – British National Formulary – A compendium of prescribing information for *all* prescription medicines available in the UK

BRICK – The term used to define a specific geographical area – usually correlating to a post code, or *group* of post codes

CALL RATE – A universal measure of how many doctors a representative is able to access over a fixed time period

CARE – 'Cholesterol And Recurrent Events' study (statin study carried out by Bristol Myers Squibb Pharmaceuticals)

CHD – Coronary Heart Disease

CLINICAL ASSISTANT – A GP who works in a hospital alongside a consultant in a specialist therapy area.

COVERAGE – The measure of *how many* different target customers you are able to access across your territory

COMPLIANCE – Refers to how well patients adhere to dosing schedules of treatments prescribed by doctors - the greater the compliance is, the better

CPD – Continuing Professional Development – A term commonly used in the NHS to describe the process of 'lifelong learning' for GPs

DETAILING – A term used to describe the process of selling product benefits to a customer

DETAIL AID – Information booklet which is used as a reference/selling aid in the process of detailing

DoH or DH – Department of Health – The body who provide strategic leadership to the NHS and social care organisations in England.

EFFICACY – This is the measure of effectiveness of a drug – therefore the greater a drug's efficacy is, the more successful it will be at treating a condition

ETMS – Electronic Territory Management System – A database of customer information used by medical representatives

FREQUENCY – The measure of *how often* you are able to access individual customers

GMS – General Medical Services – The standard medical services offered by UK GPs

GP – General Practitioner – A doctor of general medicine who works in primary care

GPSi – GP with Special interest – A doctor who practices general medicine, but who also has a specialist clinical area of interest

HDM – Healthcare Development Manager – pharmaceutical sales professional who is responsible for liaising with PCT and NHS officials to drive product endorsement at a high level

HEADCOUNT REPRESENTATIVE – a representative who is employed directly by a drug manufacturer, as opposed to a contract sales organisation

INN – International Non-proprietary Name – the standard internationally recognised name of a chemical ingredient of a drug

IN-PATIENTS – Patients who are admitted to stay in hospital wards either in emergency situations, or for scheduled procedures

KOL – Key Opinion Leader – Prescribing clinicians whose opinions are sought after due to their high level of expertise within a particular therapy area

MHRA – Medicines and Healthcare products Regulatory Agency – a branch of the Department of Health who are responsible for promoting public health and patient safety by ensuring that medicines, healthcare products and medical equipment meet basic standards of safety, quality, performance and effectiveness

MIMS – Monthly Index of Medical Specialities – a directory which outlines the main prescribing information for all UK prescription medicines. It is updated monthly to reflect new products and new drug indications, and is also available in electronic format

NEJM – New England Journal of Medicine – A highly reputable medical journal read by healthcare professionals in the UK

NHS – National Health Service – The organisation responsible for providing healthcare to the population

NICE – National Institute for Health and Clinical Excellence – The body responsible for providing national guidance on the promotion of good health and the prevention and treatment of ill health

OTC – Over The Counter - Refers to medicines which are available to be purchased by patients without the need for a doctor's prescription

OUT-PATIENTS – Patients who visit a hospital for a single follow up appointment – usually via an out-patients clinic

PA – Prescribing Adviser, or Pharmaceutical Adviser – NHS professionals who are responsible for managing drug prescribing budgets at Primary Care Trust level

PACT – Prescribing Analysis and CosT data – A quarterly analysis document sent to GPs which highlights their individual prescribing performance versus local and national averages

PCG – Primary Care Group – These were formed in 1999, but have now been superseded by the formation of PCTs

PCO – Primary Care Organisation – A genericised term which refers to the formation of a geographically formed primary healthcare network such as a PCG or PCT

PCT – Primary Care Trusts – Free standing legal entities who are managed by strategic health authorities. They have been set up around the country to fund, plan and provide health services for residents within specified geographical boundaries. There are currently 301 PCTs in England

PI – Parallel Import – A medicine which has been imported into the UK from an overseas supplier

PMCPA - Prescription Medicines Code of Practice Authority – The organisation who administers the ABPI code of practice in the UK

POM – Prescription Only Medication – A medicine which is only able to be issued to a patient on the authority of a signed prescription

QOF – Quality and Outcomes Framework – The set of clinical and organisational standards which underpin the new GMS contract for GPs

RBM – Regional Business Manager – Pharmaceutical professionals who are responsible for managing a cross-geographical team of medical sales representatives

RPC – Reply Paid Card – A postcard/flyer which offers a healthcare professional an inexpensive gift or clinical item. The term 'reply-paid' refers to the fact that postage of such flyers is pre-paid by the pharmaceutical company who issue it

RSA – Regional Sales Analysis – Local sales data which is collected from wholesalers, to track the supply of products at brick level. This data is used extensively by pharma companies as a measure of sales success

SIGN – Scottish Intercollegiate Guidelines Network – A clinical body in Scotland who develop and disseminate clinical guidelines to aid effective medical practice

SHARED-CARE – Refers to the combined care agreements between two institutions – usually hospitals and GPs

STATINS – A class of drugs used to improve heart disease by reducing systemic levels of cholesterol

StHA – Strategic Health Authority – They manage PCTs locally and are a key link between the Department of Health and the NHS. They are responsible for developing strategies, ensuring high quality performance, and building capacity in the local health service. There are currently 28 of them in England

TARGET LIST – A consolidated list of prescribing customers who are deemed as having a greater propensity to prescribe a particular drug or class of drug

TBM – Territory Business Manager – Alternative title for a primary care medical representative

TSM – Territory Sales Manager - alternative title for a primary care medical representative

WOSCOPS – 'West Of Scotland Coronary Prevention Study' (statin study carried out by Bristol Myers Squibb Pharmaceuticals)

REFERENCES

1. *'Code of Practice for the Pharmaceutical Industry'* 2006 – Prescription Medicines Code of Practice Authority: www.pmcpa.org.uk

2. *'Update on growth in prescription volume and cost year to September 2005'* Prescription Pricing Authority January 2006: www.ppa.org.uk

3. Axis Development: www.axis-development.co.uk

4. *'Practice Based Commissioning: Engaging Practices in Commissioning'* Department Of Health, 5/10/2004: www.dh.gov.uk

5. *'Why do GPs see representatives?'* November 2004: doctors.net.uk

6. *'Framework For A New Community Pharmacy Contract'* July 2003, RCGP Summary Paper 2003/13: www.rcgp.org.uk

7. *'Dawn of a new era for pharmacy'* 1st April 2005, Department Of Health: www.dh.gov.uk

8. 4S Group, The Lancet 1994; 344: 1383-89

9. Shepherd et. al, New England Journal of Medicine 1995; 333: 1301-7

10. Sacks et. al. New England Journal of Medicine 1996; 335: 1001-9

11. National Institute for Health and Clinical Excellence: www.nice.org.uk

12. 'Wellard's Guide to the NHS and Medicines' 2002 – Peter Merry.

Printed in the United Kingdom
by Lightning Source UK Ltd.
111649UKS00001B/27